Connections

A GUIDE TO USING SUPPORT
IN ACA RECOVERY

Connections
A GUIDE TO USING SUPPORT IN ACA RECOVERY

This ACA WSO Publication is under fellowship review, with a goal of eventual conference approval. Fellowship comments are invited. To submit feedback, please visit:
http://litreview.adultchildren.org

**Adult Children Of Alcoholics®/
Dysfunctional Families**

Copyright © 2025 by

Adult Children of Alcoholics®
World Service Organization, Inc.
Post Office Box 811
Lakewood, California USA 90714
www.adultchildren.org

All rights reserved. No part of this publication may be reproduced, stored in a retrieval system or transmitted in any form or by any means, electronic, mechanical, photocopying, recording, or otherwise, without the written permission of the publisher.

Adult Children of Alcoholics®/Dysfunctional Families

Connections

ISBN 978-1-944840-77-8

First Edition, First Printing, 2025

Printed in Latvia

1 2 3 4 5 6   30 29 28 27 26 25

Contents

Opening Meditation (adapted from Tradition 9) iv

Introduction 1
    The Importance of Anonymity 6
    A Note on Stylistic Choices: 7

Chapter 1: The Range of Ways to Support Each Other in ACA Recovery
    Meetings 9
    Working in a Small Group (Steps, Traits, Reparenting, etc.) 10
    Recovery Friends, Recovery Network 12
    Service Roles and Service Support 12
    Working One-to-One with Someone with Similar Experience 13
    Working Short-Term One-to-One with a Mentor 14
    Working One-to-One with Someone with More Experience 14
    A Special Note About Remote Support 15

Chapter 2: Support in Different Types of Program Work 19
    A New Hope 19
    Ready, Set, Go!! (RSG) 20
    Step Work 20
    Laundry Lists Workbook 21
    Feelings Work 22
    Reparenting Work 23
    Boundary Work 25
    Service Work 25
    The Traditions 27

Chapter 3: The Benefits of Support Relationships 31
    Learn Honest Communication 32
    Learn to Make Commitments and Keep Them 33
    Identify and Reclaim Feelings 35

Heal from Shame and Judgment 35
Grow in Spirituality 36
Become Responsible for Our Own Safety 38
Find our own Inner Loving Parent
and Reparent Our Inner Children 39
Build Self-Esteem 40
Learn to Support Others 41
See the Promises Come True 42

Chapter 4: Getting Started With Support 45
Gender and/or Sexual Orientation: 49
How to Find Supporters 50
First Conversation, Establishing "Terms of Recovery Work" 53

Chapter 5: Key Commitments in Support Relationships 57
Commitments Around the Meeting Process 57
Commitments About How We Share and Respond 58

Chapter 6: Potential Challenges in Support Relationships 65
Lack of Trust 65
Either Party is Not Meeting Commitments 68
Differences in Working Pace or Style 71
Feeling Uncomfortable and/or Unsafe 72
The Supporting Person May Appear as an Authority Figure
or Fixer 73
Either Party May Fall into People-Pleasing. 75

Chapter 7: For Sponsors or Those Considering Sponsorship 77
Challenges in Becoming Willing to Sponsor 78
I'm Not Ready 78
When Am I Ready to Become a Sponsor? 83

Chapter 8: Conclusion 87

Appendix A—2017 Ballot Proposal 2017-4 89

Appendix B—Affirmations for Those in Support Relationships ... 91

Appendix C—Sample Meeting Language About Finding Supporters 93

Appendix D—One Member's ACA Sponsorship Agreement 95

Appendix E—Key Recovery Goals and Milestones 99

Appendix F—The ACA Promises 101

Appendix G—The ACA Bill of Rights 103

Appendix H—How the Traditions Guide Us in Working with Another 105
Tradition One 105
Tradition Two 105

Appendix I—ACA Suggested Commitment to Service 107

Appendix J—Safety Tent Card 109

Appendix K—Introduction to ACA Workgroups 111

Creating / Joining ACA Workgroups 112
Duration 112
Group Size 112
Location 112
Format 113
Safety Guidelines 113
Experience & Expertise 113
Questions, Conflict & Authority 113

Additional Workgroup Resources for the Loving Parent Guidebook 114

ACA Workgroup Sample Safety Guidelines 115

Opening Meditation

(adapted from Tradition 9)

Higher power, may we remember that ACA and its meeting and service structure are different from our families of origin. May we be patient and avoid reaching for the easiest way out when confronted with a difficult situation. Help us and those supporting us in the ACA program to ask for help in keeping our relationship safe and recovery-oriented. Also, help us celebrate the things that we do right.

INTRODUCTION

This Guide was written to address a motion passed by ACA delegates in 2017 that read:

We propose that the WSO revise BRB chapter 11 and the sponsorship pamphlet for clarity and consistency.

(See Appendix A for the full ballot proposal.)

One inconsistency was that chapter 11 of *Adult Children of Alcoholics Alcoholic/Dysfunctional Families* (called the *Big Red Book* or the BRB) recommends the "fellow traveler method of sponsorship," but then describes traditional sponsorship. We know that since the book was written in 2006, most ACA members have used the term "fellow traveler" to mean two people sharing their program and life experiences back and forth equally and the terms "sponsor-sponsee" to mean a relationship where the sponsee shares program or life experiences and the sponsor listens and offers loving feedback.

A working group was set up to resolve this inconsistency, which resulted in strong opinions about whether "fellow travelers" or "sponsorship" was the better form of support relationship and what term could encompass both types of relationship. After two years, the working group agreed to use the general term "support" as an umbrella term for any relationship between ACAs who work together on recovery. In addition, the working group realized that presenting the range of ways to support others in recovery required more than revising chapter 11 of the BRB. That is why we ultimately wrote this Guide, which is being submitted to the Big Red Book Revision Working Group to include in their revision process.

The term "support" is not a substitute for "fellow travelers," "sponsorship," or any other term members use for support relationships. It is designed to show that in all support relationships, one person shares their experience openly and honestly, learning to trust the other, and the other person listens intently with love and uses the voice of the inner loving parent in responding to the person sharing. In any support relationship, the goal is the same: honest communication and loving feedback resulting in growth in recovery for both people.

We use the term "sharing person" for those who share their recovery experience with a supporting person. The word "supporting person" includes anyone who listens intently and gently and lovingly helps another person in recovery, holding space without judgment. The term "support" includes sponsors, co-sponsors, fellow travelers, recovery partners, sharing partners, recovery coaches, and work group members. Using an umbrella term helps us see the commonalities in support relationships. Again, these terms are for ease of reference in this Guide. In your support relationship, please use the term that works best for you.

SHARE

In almost six years of ACA, I have never had a sponsor, nor been a sponsor. I have done my deepest recovery work as part of small, intensive workgroups. It is mostly through these groups that I have met my closest recovery partners (what some might call co-sponsors) who I meet up with or speak to by phone at least weekly.

SHARE

Some call me sponsor, some call me fellow traveler, some call me elder, some call me a friend. For me, it isn't the label that is important. What is important is what are they looking for. How can I be of service in a healthy way, and is this something that calls my heart? The term "sponsorship" is simply a verb asking us to give and/or receive ACA recovery support.

As we grow in recovery, the nature of our support relationships may change. We remember that we may not all be of equal experience in program, but we are all on equal footing—human beings deserving of love and respect.

Above all, support is a spiritual process. Asking for help is scary. As a supporting person, we must heal our ACA trait of fixing or rescuing. We avoid being an authority figure and choose gentle honesty over people-pleasing. If in doubt, we check with our own support network. We remember that ACAs long to be heard. We all suffered a loss of trust as children. Rebuilding trust takes time. We are patient and kind. When we are the sharing person, we risk coming out of isolation. We build self-esteem by believing we are worthy of support in recovery. We practice being honest and vulnerable. These characteristics affect all support relationships.

SHARE

When I think about sponsorship now, I think of "someone who cares" because that is one of the meanings of the word that we use for a sponsor in our [Lithuanian] language ("globėjas"). As a newcomer, I was in dreadful fear of trusting anyone and felt a lot of resentment towards higher power. Now, I see him as the ultimate sponsor of nurturing my happiness because in ACA I have healed a lot of anger and had many inspirations towards spirituality while working the program that changed my life. I see sponsorship (or "healthy care and walk together") as one of the most enriching experiences in life and I am thankful for the profound changes ACA can make to the life of the fellow traveler. And God wants to be a fellow traveler as well together in my life. How would I know? Because step 3 talks about care, and if somebody cares for us deeply, that is love.

This Guide is not designed to help ACAs connect with a sponsor or other support person, although we make suggestions about how and where support can be found. We know there is a lack of members offering to sponsor. chapter 7 of the *Big Red Book* is directed to sponsors or those thinking of becoming sponsors. We urge you to keep an open mind. Sponsorship is less about years in recovery or knowledge of the ACA program and more about being a loving presence and guide. Our past wounds may cause us to either resist trusting someone who seeks to guide us or to reject help, thinking we must find the perfect person, one who would never hurt or disappoint us. The bedrock of our ACA program is love. If we seek and offer support with love, we will begin to heal our childhood wounds.

SHARE

Growing up in family dysfunction, one of my deepest wounds is trust. I was taught not to trust myself, and thus, I had nothing to gauge trust with others. Yet, I needed to come out of my emotional isolation and connect with others to heal in ACA recovery. Sponsorship didn't work for me, as my authority issues ran too deep. I'm grateful I've been able to connect with others deeply in ACA to rebuild trust outside the traditional sponsor/sponsee model.

Most of this Guide will apply to all support relationships, whether they are called sponsorship, co-sponsorship, recovery partners, fellow travelers, or something else. We present the benefits to our recovery of all types of support relationships and how to handle common challenges in all support relationships. Chapter 7 of this Guide addresses those considerations unique to sponsorship, including the challenge of people being willing to sponsor.

Many of us ACAs are rule followers and are motivated by a sense of urgency. Therefore, when we read the statement in the *Big Red Book* that says, "Get a sponsor," we think that we must find a sponsor immediately. In part, this is a holdover from the AA program, which tells newcomers they should get a sponsor immediately to stay sober. We offer to ACA members that when our program suggests we get a sponsor, it actually means to come out of isolation and find support—not necessarily one person—to guide us through the program.

The ACA Solution says, "We use the steps, we use the meetings, we use the telephone." The Newcomer welcome suggests that we proceed slowly and deliberately. We suggest newcomers attend six meetings before even deciding if the ACA program is right for them. The most important thing we have discovered in talking to people who both offer and receive support in ACA is that coming out of isolation is an important first step. This can be as simple as turning to the person next to you in a meeting and saying, "I really liked what you said. May I call you?"

We know ACA lacks enough people willing to be sponsors in our program, and therefore newcomers may feel frustrated. However, we believe that support is available in many different ways, and that once we open our eyes to the many possibilities of support in the ACA program, we will begin a long and happy journey toward recovery. We offer this Guide in the spirit of gentleness, humor, love, and respect.

Meditation

May I embrace my fellow travelers, standing shoulder-to-shoulder, heart-to-heart, spirit-to-spirit, and show gratitude for this program.

The Importance of Anonymity

We believe that the support relationship requires confidentiality and anonymity—in both the content of what is shared and the identity of the supporting and sharing person. See the section below on "Traditions."

Meditation

Grant me the ability to see the connecting thread that anonymity brings to the ACA program and have the willingness to practice ACA principles instead of a false self-personality. May I feel safe as I share my story with another person in ACA. May I put principles before personalities by remembering the purpose of this relationship.

Introduction

A Note on Stylistic Choices:

This Guide has adopted several style decisions regarding terms. If these don't work for you, we encourage you to use the terms that do work for you.

1. We acknowledge that not all ACA members use the pronouns "he" or "she." We use "they" as a singular pronoun rather than "he or she" to make the text gender-neutral, except in shares by ACA members.

2. We do not capitalize "higher power" to support the spiritual, not religious, nature of the ACA program. ACA supports each of us to find a higher power of our understanding. Some of us choose to call a higher power by traditional religious names or by terms such as universe, spirit, etc. Others may use no name at all or choose a secular force, such as the love and wisdom of their recovery community. By using the neutral term "higher power," we intend to support each person's unique spiritual journey.

3. We have used a number of different words to introduce a prayer or meditation throughout this Guide. For example, sometimes a meditation begins: "Higher power grant that I may." Sometimes, we say, "Higher power may I." Sometimes, we do not begin the prayer/meditation with the words higher power at all. We encourage you to find the method that works best for you and to use that in your reading of this Guide.

4. We offer a list of "milestones or goals" (Appendix E). Milestones and goals differ from affirmations. (Appendix B) Milestones/goals are stated in the language of accomplishment to recognize progress in recovery. Affirmations are statements of the behavior we intend to bring forth in our lives.

5. Some shares have been edited for length or clarity. We use an ellipsis [...] to indicate where material has been edited from a share for length. We have kept references in shares to program terms and materials the way members wrote them rather than changing them to the style used in this Guide. We thank all who submitted shares about their experience with support.

6. This Guide is not designed to connect individual ACA members with a supporting person. Rather, it is designed to show different methods and places where support can be found. In this respect, we hope to demystify and alleviate the fear that keeps some ACA members from volunteering to help and others from asking for help. We are all equal in deserving love and respect.

CHAPTER 1
THE RANGE OF WAYS TO SUPPORT EACH OTHER IN ACA RECOVERY

THE FOLLOWING PRESENTS a range of ways to find support in recovery. We begin at the newcomer stage, where we simply attend meetings and then go on to address relationships as we progress in program. Having a range of relationships to choose from allows us to work our program with gentleness, humor, love, and respect.

Meetings

Most of us find early support from others in meetings. Many meetings keep lists of phone numbers or ask if members are seeking phone numbers, a fellow traveler, a sponsor, or other support. Those who attend meetings that focus on the steps or other program materials may find in sharing that they particularly relate to another member's share and will continue the conversation after a meeting. Social activities, for example, anniversary meetings, coffee groups, lunch clubs, or other group social activities with members, are another way we can practice our new-found recovery behaviors.

SHARE

It took me a while to pick up the phone and call ACAs who had given me their number. But a few months into the program, I found myself bonded to my critical parent. I reached out to a person around whom I felt comfortable. They didn't answer, but leaving the message already gave me some space. When they called back, and I heard the care in their voice, I teared up. Being able to talk to someone who understood helped me avoid hours of spinning in a shame spiral. I've never once regretted picking up the phone, but I've many times wished that I picked up the phone sooner.

Working in a Small Group (Steps, Traits, Reparenting, etc.)

Some ACAs join private groups that aren't registered as open ACA meetings to work the program. These groups often meet to complete a cycle of the *Twelve Steps of Adult Children* workbook or other ACA workbooks. These members provide each other with support as they mutually engage in program work.

SHARE

When the Yellow ACA Steps Workbook came out, I and a fellow ACA member decided to take our steps together. We both had roughly the same amount of time in the fellowship. We called each other co-sponsors or fellow travelers ... We gave feedback only when asked to do so. Mainly, we practiced active listening to each other's responses.

Some ACAs choose to work primarily in small groups; others combine small group work with working one-to-one with other adult children. Frequently, members will meet someone in a small group who then becomes a fellow traveler, co-sponsor, or sponsor. The ACA program offers choice and encourages creativity in how members find support.

The *Big Red Book* states that the traits we developed to cope with dysfunction in childhood "cause us to recreate our family of origin in our adult relationships." This can occur anywhere, and study groups are no exception. Working with ACA literature can bring up buried memories and triggers. We might find ourselves or others playing out a familiar family role or responding from our wounded inner child or inner teenager.

Small groups strive to create safety for members. Even so, members can become triggered by one another and dysfunctional behaviors can arise. It is not uncommon for a member to leave a workgroup along the way. We might realize that a particular group isn't a good match or that small group work isn't a good fit for us at the time. It's okay to leave groups and meetings that don't work for us and find ones that do. Finding a group that fits is a process and can take time.

Study groups give us an opportunity to practice healthier ways of being and release outdated coping behaviors. Whenever possible, it can be helpful to have an ACA network outside the group to support you for reparenting purposes, as well as to discuss issues and feelings that arise. It's important to keep each study group a safe place to practice these new ways of being.

See Appendix K for "Introduction to ACA Workgroups," which comes from the exhibits to *A New Hope ACA Beginners Meeting Handbook*.

SHARE

Both individual and groups have been valuable. Personal relationships require time and an investment. Both require trusting the process and having a relationship with a higher power. I have learned to trust those who are trustworthy and value my personal integrity.

Recovery Friends, Recovery Network

As we progress in program, we can develop multiple relationships with friends who can answer a quick question, offer a listening ear when we have a program issue, or simply practice learning how to play and have fun in our lives. As we learn how to have honest conversations, resolve disagreements or conflict, and grow into our authentic selves, we come to rely on our network. When one person is not available to pick up the phone, another may be. We learn not to take it personally if someone is not available. We practice boundaries, learn how not to gossip, and how to respect each other's anonymity through our network.

A network gives us many options for getting our needs met. It also allows us to talk about our feelings and reactions in healthy ways with people not directly involved with our conflicts. This helps us practice healthy communication rather than codependence.

Service Roles and Service Support

By taking on responsibilities in service, as greeter, chair, meeting secretary, intergroup representative or the like, we meet others in recovery and learn to practice responsibility, which increases our self-esteem. Attending business meetings provides a place to be heard and practice group conscience with others. As we grow in recovery, we may volunteer service at the World Service Organization (wso) level.

Many acas who perform service seek a service supporter, someone more experienced in service, to ask questions and receive support.

SHARE

One challenge I find in service sponsorship is recognizing when I am over-committed. As an ACA, I fall into the trap of trying to earn love by doing projects. This can lead to trying to control outcomes. My service sponsor helps me see where I might need to cut back on commitments or where I am trying to manipulate an outcome instead of relying on group conscience.

Working One-to-One with Someone with Similar Experience

In this approach, two ACA members with similar experience, strength, and hope in program (which we refer to as experience) support each other's continued recovery. This support relationship is frequently called fellow travelers. This model works well for ACA members with significant experience because they will be familiar with program literature and principles. This can also work for two relative newcomers, although it seems to work best if at least one of the newcomers has some experience in another 12 step recovery program. Also, it helps to identify a more experienced ACA who is available to answer questions or lend support.

In these relationships, the roles of supporting person and sharing person shift back and forth. We learn to listen intently when the other person is sharing, avoid giving advice unless it is directly requested, and practice the gentle and loving language used by a loving parent. We may establish a set amount of time for each person to share so that they feel fully heard.

🪷 Meditation

Higher power, may I walk hand-in-hand with my fellow traveler so we can help each other recover on the less-traveled road.

Working Short-Term One-to-One with a Mentor

Some groups have created a mentoring program designed to provide one-to-one support to newcomers in their first few weeks in ACA and introduce them to the program.

A mentor aspires to answer questions, help a newcomer establish a recovery network, and explain the elements of different types of program work.

Working One-to-One with Someone with More Experience

In this approach, one person with more experience works with someone less experienced. This is the method of support most frequently called sponsorship. Most of the information in chapter 11 of the *Big Red Book* addresses one-to-one sponsorship by someone with more experience of someone with less experience.

Both the more experienced and the less experienced members can grow in trust and intimacy as the relationship develops. The experienced member shares their experience and guides the newcomer in building their own foundation for recovery. These experienced members are not therapists or counselors, but they can offer needed support to another person revisiting abuse, trauma, and other overwhelming childhood experiences.

In this support relationship, the more experienced member works their program with their own recovery network. They keep their focus on the sharing person's recovery.

SHARE

Regarding the term "fellow traveler"—to me, a sponsor is more than a fellow traveler. A sponsor is a spiritual mentor who makes me look at things I may not have looked at before and is not afraid to gently convey the need to take an honest look at myself. I feel safe with my sponsor, as this person is careful not to be critical of my pain but understanding of it.

A Special Note About Remote Support

As we come out of isolation and begin to work with others on our recovery, some members prefer face-to-face meetings or conversations with others. Others, for reasons of comfort, distance from meetings, or personal preference, choose to meet on the telephone, online, or through electronic means. All forms of support work can be accomplished remotely. Members can use mail, email, telephone, and video conferencing services to do extensive program work with long-distance support.

SHARE

I'm currently completing the 12 steps one-to-one through the telephone with a trusted fellow traveler. Speaking to my fellow traveler honestly about my difficulties helps me realize I am worthy of love and support, no matter what I've been through or done. Hearing another relate to stories I've felt so much shame about grants me the opportunity to feel more compassion for myself and others. I can feel safe practicing vulnerability with an individual who has been through similar experiences as me.

SHARE

Personally, my best recovery work was done over a lengthy lunch in a Cape Town restaurant after our Saturday meeting. We kept it up for 9 years, and it was where I experienced the "fellow traveler" concept in action, where we each just spoke about what was coming up for us, either after the meeting or in our life in general. There was no advice-giving, but a lot of ESH (Experience, Strength, and Hope) shared, lots of tears, some laughter, and a strong sense of support and unconditional, non-judgmental acceptance.

This was SO different from my experience in my family of origin or even another 12 step fellowship I had been part of. I became very aware that I, like most adult children I have met over my now almost 20 years in the program, tend to alternate in varying degrees between compliant and defiant when confronted with anything that vaguely feels like an authority figure. Respectful equality was the thing I had to learn how to live, and this was where I got to practice it in action, with others struggling with a similar challenge.

I no longer live in South Africa, and I miss those lunches to this day, but they helped me build a solid ACA recovery foundation. Their value in helping me understand and work my program lives on in my heart, mind, and life, and the warmth of those connections to what I now think of as my ACA family is something I will treasure for the rest of my life.

I am also profoundly grateful for the internet because I am today still doing a closed study group—LPG this time—with another of my fellow travelers who still lives in South Africa. And in my service work at an international level, I have yet to meet in person those [whom] I work most closely with, but they too have become family of the heart, and a treasured part of my ACA family.

CHAPTER 2
SUPPORT IN DIFFERENT TYPES OF PROGRAM WORK

ALL TYPES OF PROGRAM WORK profit by sharing with supporters. Some of these types of work will naturally precede others. For example, the meeting format A New Hope and the introductory workshop Ready, Set, Go!! are designed for newcomers. Other work, such as feelings work, step work, laundry list trait work, reparenting, grief work and family-of-origin work, may be done in a different order. It can be helpful for those new to ACA to first understand the options and then explore what works for us.

A New Hope
This is a meeting format designed for newcomers to introduce them to the fundamentals of ACA recovery. *A New Hope ACA Beginners Meeting Handbook* was released in fellowship review in 2024 toward the process of becoming ACA Conference Approved Literature. It can be read alone or as

part of meetings that use the format. See Appendix K for an Introduction to ACA Workgroups, which is an exhibit to *A New Hope*.

Ready, Set, Go!! (RSG)

This program has been developed to introduce people to ACA, to the steps, and to the inner child over a short period. It can also be used as a refresher for more experienced members. RSG is designed in different lengths: a one-day RSG event, a five-week face-to-face RSG meeting, or a six-week RSG online or telephone meeting.

RSG has an option of using a sharing partner for the 5- or 6-week sessions.

Step Work

Chapter 7 of the *Big Red Book* contains the step program, which some meetings use for their format. The step program also appears in a workbook called *Twelve Steps of Adult Children* (often referred to as the *Twelve Steps Yellow Workbook*). This workbook contains questions and reflections about the steps. Some adult children join meetings that read the *Twelve Steps Yellow Workbook*. You can find these meetings at http://adultchildren.org/meeting-search under "Meeting Format Filter."

Other members join a small group that works the *Twelve Steps Yellow Workbook* over a set number of weeks. Still others work through the workbook one-to-one, either with someone of similar experience or with someone with more experience. When working the workbook with someone with more experience, the focus is on the answers and reflections of the person working the twelve steps. Many members find it helpful to revisit their answers in subsequent sessions, assessing their growth in the program as they go.

SHARE

When I first came into the program, I was extremely fortunate to be invited into a 20-week Yellow Book step study group. The group had an experienced leader who skillfully kept the sizable group safe and on task ... Listening to other's stories, I found deep compassion bubbling up for people I previously would have avoided because of my laundry list traits. Because of many of their shares, I was able to recognize and face much of the childhood trauma and abandonment I had been denying, and I began to find some self-compassion.

Laundry Lists Workbook

The *Laundry Lists Workbook, Integrating Our Laundry Lists Traits*, takes an in-depth look at the traits from a variety of angles. Although it can be used at any stage of program work, some members find the material easier to digest and explore once they have worked the ACA 12 steps and/or done some reparenting work. Others find the perspective they gain from working the *Laundry Lists Workbook* helps them recognize and release, heal, or integrate laundry list traits. This workbook also addresses the "flip side" of laundry list traits, for example, examining where we may have become an authority figure.

As with the *Step Workbook*, the *Laundry Lists Workbook* is used in a variety of settings, including meetings. You can find these meetings at http://adultchildren.org/meeting-search and using the "Meeting Format Filter."

We can also work on identifying and addressing our laundry list traits in all our program work with supporters by identifying which trait is triggered in a moment, which traits cause problems in our life overall, and learning to balance or release them.

Feelings Work

When we begin in ACA, we may not have access to our feelings. We learn that the return of feelings is a sign that healing has begun.

We may share feelings without asking for comment; our supporting person may ask us what we are feeling as we tell our story; or they may provide feedback or mirroring of feelings. As we recover, we can feel grief, anger, sorrow, fear, guilt, joy, playfulness, love and serenity or more.

Some ACAs who are not familiar with their feelings turn to sources outside of ACA, such as a therapist or outside reading about healing. Mindfulness meditation can also support feelings work by helping us learn to ground our attention in the body.

SHARE

I started to receive requests from other ACA members to hear their 4th step after they had completed a step study; others needed support with grieving their feelings, healing, and integrating the laundry lists or connecting with the inner child and reparenting. They had heard me share my experience and recovery in meetings.

Meditation

May I find the courage to reach out to a fellow traveler, the strength to express my true feelings, and the wisdom to know my feelings will not kill me.

Reparenting Work

We can work on reparenting skills in a variety of ways. We can work through chapter 8 of the *Big Red Book*, "Becoming Your Own Loving Parent;" we may attend telephone or in-person meetings that address reparenting. We may also work through the *Loving Parent Guidebook* in an open meeting or closed study group. You can find these meetings at http://adultchildren.org/meeting-search and clicking on "Meeting Format Filter."

Guidance for working the *Loving Parent Guidebook* in a closed ACA group and one-to-one is offered in the *Loving Parent Guidebook's* appendix, along with a suggested group format script. A https://adultchildren.org/literature/loving-parent-Guidebook/ you can click on "LPG Study Group Tips and Sample Materials" to find formats for studying the book.

It helps to do reparenting work with someone who has experience with reparenting and family-of-origin grief work. Others, such as spiritual advisers, can support reparenting work.

SHARE

A season, a reason, or a lifetime. Not all my ACA recovery partners over the years have remained close fellow travelers—there have been times when recovery paths diverged. When this happens, my abandonment (or abandoner/rescuer) issues can get triggered. I can easily go to shame or blame. Through reparenting, I tell my inner child, "It's OK ... even though other people in our life may come and go, I will always love you and be with you."

Reparenting work involves identifying the inner child or children. We learn how to hear and validate our inner child or children. We identify the age of our inner children as they react to a trigger. We see how our inner children feel when they are triggered. As we learn how to understand the inner family's needs and how to develop a cooperation between adult and child, we find the spirit of joy that inhabits every child.

SHARE

Sometimes, we've had what I would call reparenting brainstorming sessions, where my sponsor helps me figure out what I could do to take care of my inner children or connect with my inner loving parent. Through these conversations, I've done things like buy coloring books, watercolors, crayons, and a Mad Libs book. I've also begun creating a loving parent voice and character within myself through suggestions from my sponsor. Sometimes, we play and laugh by doing Mad Libs, and that's been really nice.

Boundary Work

We learn the important process of setting boundaries. This includes identifying issues with boundaries, such as the absence of or confusion around boundaries or boundary violations. We also learn about the need for boundaries, and how to practice and support identifying and setting boundaries.

To establish an inner foundation for boundaries, members might attend an ACA meeting on boundaries. You can find these meetings at http://adultchildren.org/meeting-search by clicking on "Search Text Filter" and typing in the word "boundaries."

We can also review and work through chapter 13 of *The Loving Parent Guidebook: Setting Internal Boundaries: An Expression of Unconditional Love*. Working with supporters who have learned to set and uphold boundaries can be particularly helpful.

Service Work

Whenever we are in a support relationship as a supporting person, we are performing service. We extend our time, attention, and experience as a loving form of service to another ACA. When we chair a meeting, volunteer to lead a business meeting, or handle getting literature for our meeting, we are also doing service. Volunteering to do service is an opportunity to support each other around issues that arise in groups. The Suggested Commitment to

Service (See Appendix I) guides our groups, service structure, and recovery relationships so that we perform service and practice our recovery together. Others may benefit from our service, and we deepen our own recovery.

Serving in a meeting, intergroup, region, and/or at the World Service Organization of ACA helps carry the message of recovery. We may also act as a support for new groups and their trusted servants when appropriate.

Two ACAs may support each other by carrying out service, either for the first time or moving from one type of service to another. Encouragement from a fellow who has been involved in service can make the path clearer.

We recommend that any ACA member who takes on a service role find a service supporter. This can be one's regular supporter or a separate person supporting service on specific projects at the meeting, intergroup, region, and WSO levels. Service support involves the traditions, concepts, and service commitments of ACA. We may also seek help resolving conflict or getting support to have difficult conversations in a kind and loving way. Service support works best if the supporting person has experience in service.

By giving service, we add to our ACA recovery program, expanding from an individual level of healing to include a group level of healing.

This is a safe place to start practicing our ACA recovery tools with groups before venturing too far into the outside world. Our service supporter can guide us to integrate both our individual and group ACA recovery experiences.

We learn to provide healthy service so that ACA can continue to carry the message to the adult child and support our fellowship. This is a type of ACA recovery that deepens our healing, and the benefits flow into our personal and work communities. We integrate our self-care, set healthy boundaries, and balance practices.

Meditation

Higher power, may I be a trusted servant seeking to support the welfare of the support relationship. May I remember that the life of my program and my own recovery depend upon my willingness to put the support relationship's welfare above my own will. May I always practice unity.

SHARE

Anytime I support another ACA member, it also supports my recovery with increased insights, clarity, and deep healing. I share my recovery and service recovery experience with what I have learned for myself and what I might be doing differently in the future, knowing what I know now. I find assessing with gentleness on where I am in the feelings, where am I in the steps, where I am in the laundry lists, connecting with my inner child, and reparenting is my pathway. One baby step at a time has been key for me.

The Traditions

The Twelve Traditions of ACA (see Appendix G) guide our groups and our service structure, outlining fellowship unity, group autonomy, and the authority of a higher power in our group consciences.

The benefits of using the Traditions extend to our whole lives. They give us a roadmap for living, which can improve our relationships. We develop boundaries and mutual respect. This results in healthier groups and business meetings. Our service work and communities benefit, as well.

🪷 Meditation

Higher power, I seek a loving voice in this supportive connection. May I remember that the life of my program and, therefore, my own recovery depends upon my willingness to put the welfare of the support relationship above my will. Where I disagree with the view of my support partner, may I state my case honestly and respectfully. May I listen to and consider my support partner's views.

We can study the Traditions with the support of someone more experienced, someone with a similar level of experience, or in a study group.

SHARE

I connect the acts of caring and nurturing that I receive and give with what it means to be loved and supported by a parent or a family member. My biological family may not be or never have been as supportive and caring as I need, and today, that is ok because I have my own family now and my sponsors and sponsees are at the heart of it.

SHARE

I first got a service sponsor when I joined the WSO in a service position. I had had a prior service role as the chair of the last in-person world conference in Malmo, Sweden, and that gave me a taste of some of the issues that can come up in service. I realized it would be a good idea to have someone I could ask for help, particularly when I couldn't achieve a group conscience or found conflict in a meeting.

Since then, I have had a service sponsor and have also become a service sponsor to others. As a service sponsor myself, I don't talk about ACA recovery in general. It's important to me to keep recovery issues separate from service issues. My approach to being a service sponsor and working with a service sponsor is to ground our conversations in the traditions and the concepts. That helps resolve most issues that come up for me.

When I am emotional or I find others becoming emotional, I know it's time to use the principles of the program and become reflective about what is going on. If I'm helping someone who is having problems in a business meeting, I might suggest that they simply step back, stop talking, and become an observer of what is going on in the meeting. I also remind them that it's not their responsibility to save a committee or a group. The question for me is to remember the goal is what's for the good of ACA, not what I want myself.

Am I taking on too much by forcing solutions? When I find myself trying to force solutions, I need to ask, what is for the best for ACA? I need to take my ego out of it.

For me, the inner child has no place in a business meeting. The inner child is important in personal recovery but not in business meetings because the inner child feels emotions and I try to keep emotion out of my service work. It's so rewarding being both a sponsor and a service sponsor because it's the same principle: I can't give away what I don't have. It's a reminder for me that what's important is to go back to basics.

CHAPTER 3
THE BENEFITS OF SUPPORT RELATIONSHIPS

MOST OF THE SUPPORT RELATIONSHIPS discussed in chapter 1 of this Guide involve sharing back and forth, where each party alternates being the supporting person or the sharing person. Even in relationships such as mentor or sponsor, the supporting person often reports that their program is greatly improved by supporting another. In this section, we look at the benefits of support to both parties in a support relationship.

Anyone who identifies with the laundry list traits of the adult child soon sees that recovery requires reading, introspection, retrieving childhood stories, a diligent attempt to heal past wounds, and finding the loving voice of an inner parent to help the wounded inner child.

In working with supporters, we review the laundry lists to see which trait(s) might be activated. We examine what false beliefs and childhood conditioning might be coloring our perspective or creating distorted thinking.

Learn Honest Communication

Our disease is one of isolation. We learned as children to keep secrets and not to trust or tell what was going on in our homes. Coming out of isolation is painful, but in program, we soon realize we are not alone. Doing family-of-origin work shows us the cost of being unable to speak freely and honestly. As we work with supporters, we develop these skills. We learn to trust that another person genuinely wants to help us and knows how we feel.

Working with a supporter or in a group requires that we come out of isolation. We realize that we are not alone—in the world or as a person who grew up in a dysfunctional family. We also come out of denial—whether that is about the true nature of our childhood wounds, our codependency with others, or our true feelings. We uncover denial slowly and gently, trusting that we will discover what we need to know when the time is right to handle it.

We begin to see our history of codependent relationships and how they no longer serve us. As ACAs, we have suffered too long with failed relationships. The immediate benefit of working with a supporter is that we break this cycle. We allow someone else into our true lives. We come out of isolation and denial. We learn to ask for and accept help.

Honest communication means we avoid people-pleasing and agreeing with someone just to avoid conflict.

SHARE

I was in my mid-30s, and my first marriage was coming to an end. I had spent my whole life withholding any inner pain from others. Don't talk, don't trust, don't feel.

But on that day, I told my ACA sponsor exactly how I felt. Then I cried with my eyes shut. As I sobbed, I heard his gentle voice: "Just let it out." I sobbed some more. "Just let it out," he said. By the time my crying quieted, something changed in me. My marriage was still ending, but I felt loved and supported and assured that I would be OK if I kept my focus on recovery.

Meditation

Grant that I may practice new, trusting behavior with my fellow travelers, learning healthier ways of communicating that will keep me from leaving others for the wrong reasons.

Learn to Make Commitments and Keep Them

When we ask someone or a group to support us, we realize that we can ask for help and accept it. When we agree on a program of recovery, we learn to make commitments and keep them. We learn to show up for ourselves and be more genuine with others.

As we work with one another, we make commitments to meet, write, and share. Often, the supporter may see parts of their program that could be strengthened. Working with another can reveal gaps in one's program that need attention.

If commitments are not being honored, we learn to say what we mean and how to not say it meanly. We did not learn how to deal with conflict as children, and we may have avoided it in recovery. We can practice how to lovingly confront issues while holding firm to program principles.

SHARE

A sister traveler I was guiding through the steps had realized after a year of traveling together that she needed someone with a different experience to guide her, someone who had knowledge or personal experience of changing violent behavior, be it physical, emotional, or verbal. I didn't have that, and my guidance for her to stand up for herself was harmful to her considering her past behavior in relationships. When she told me, I realized that my suggestion of her educating me about it was also harmful. Someone being guided doesn't need the extra burden of educating someone on the issues they are struggling with. I realized that, felt my shame, and apologized from my heart.

This parting of ways brought up mother abandonment issues and comparisons with younger, more socially connected people. I had grown up with a father that had abused his emotional power as a psychiatrist by wanting to "help" others. This included me and his much younger ex-wife (my mother). He hadn't formed equal relationships with people his own age or [dealt] with his own powerlessness that happened to be over the same challenges I was experiencing: loneliness, a lack of friends [and a] romantic partner. I had never learned healthy relating, self love, or seen my parents having close friendships.

Meditation

Higher power, help me acknowledge my recovery actions by celebrating my progress with my supporters, who support and value me.

Identify and Reclaim Feelings

Many of us have lived most of our lives feeling numb or unsure of what feelings are. We may fear that once we begin feeling, our feelings will overwhelm us. But as we share our story, identify our feelings, and relate to our supporter's experiences, we learn that we can heal the shame and judgment that may have marked our childhood. This is an important step in breaking the "don't talk, don't trust, don't feel, don't remember" pattern of childhood. We learn that our feelings will not kill us.

The support relationship is an intimate one. We are both privy to long-held secrets and shame. We learn to express our feelings of compassion without falling into people-pleasing. As we hear each other's stories, we both experience vulnerability and intimacy.

Meditation

May I practice finding my voice with another person in recovery so that when the time comes, I'll be ready to speak up for myself.

Heal from Shame and Judgment

Shame blinds us to the fact that love is inside each of us, waiting to be discovered.

When we do deep recovery work with a supporter, we each bring the vulnerability of our inner children to each other. In doing so, we heal old wounds and learn new ways to trust. When conflict arises, we remember we are both doing our best to work with our inner child parts, which gives us compassion and patience both for ourselves and our recovery partners.

SHARE

Sharing intimate details about my life with trustworthy women has been a key factor in my being able to be more of an actor than reactor in my life. Recently, I was asked to take a fellow traveler through steps 4 and 5, and we are working together on how best to do this. I can always ask a fellow traveler with more ACA experience for help with any problem I might have that is based on my ACA recovery.

Meditation

On this day, may I look at myself through the eyes of recovery, not through the eyes of my caretakers from childhood.

Grow in Spirituality

Just as we need a supporter, or supporters, to aid our recovery, we seek a connection with a higher power or with principles of spirituality. For those of us who grew up with a blaming or shaming higher power, or no higher power, learning to trust those supporting us is the first step in developing the trust necessary to depend on a loving higher power. We grow in spirituality as we hear others share their spiritual journey. We grow in tolerance as we learn that others may have a very different view of spirituality than our own.

SHARE

I was seeking my third sponsor and had finished the steps. I had lost my previous sponsor when I was seeking international support in standing up for my spiritual inclusion. I wanted to and needed to be true to my own spirituality, witchy and queer, and wanted to be able to use the words greater power where it said higher power in our texts when leading meetings and reading texts. It was especially important for me when leading meetings as a woman, reclaiming leadership in service roles in public spaces. I needed that spiritual inclusion to be present in my meetings, to feel safe enough to heal.

ACA had had its first annual business conference [ABC] outside the states in my country, Sweden. I had just experienced that in international service, there was a much greater openness for spiritual inclusion than at the physical meetings I could choose from in Sweden at the time (2019). Attending a loving parent workshop online, I noticed a radiant and joyous woman who was also in service. I mustered up my courage to ask her if she was open to discuss sponsorship/fellow traveling with me. I had learned to pray and ask for what I needed for traveling together, like being ok with me using words in line with my spirituality and the clarity and courage of seeing sexism in our world. Sexism has harmed me a lot growing up, both with my father and also being a survivor of child sexual abuse in the public library. I need to check where a possible fellow traveler stands concerning these issues before starting a possible journey together.

Our concept of and reliance on a higher power may grow. Often, it goes from resistance when we first enter recovery to a growing spiritual awareness. Working with another can give us a fresh perspective on a higher power. We come to rely on spirituality to help us when we are unsure or confused when working together. We realize that when we are in the supporting role, we are not an authority figure. The only authority figure in the support relationship is a higher power, as that higher power may reveal itself to us. We use the spiritual principles of love, honesty, trust, and respect.

SHARE

I wrote a tenth step checklist to share with supporters. It converts the spiritual principles of the program, such as being compassionate, forgiving oneself and others, saying affirmations, and acting with loving kindness, into a checklist of how I want to put those practices into my life each day. I ask supporters to identify one success and one challenge from the list, which I do as well. When I turn spiritual principles into action, I am relying on a higher power.

Our spiritual journey is enriched by asking questions and hearing about the spiritual journey of those in our support network.

SHARE

As someone who does not believe in God or a higher power, the most significant work I've done with others is assisting them in teasing out the underlying principles or teachings of the steps. This has been particularly helpful for those who struggle with the concept of a higher power or who have difficulty with the gender pronouns in the steps.

Meditation

Spirit of recovery, may I find a spiritual connection with you with the help of my supporters and the tools of ACA.

Become Responsible for Our Own Safety

Both parties in a support relationship need safety. They need to feel they can share without fearing gossip or disclosure outside the relationship. If we begin to feel uncomfortable or unsafe, we learn to speak our truth without fear. We learn to trust our intuition if we feel uncomfortable about speaking up or setting healthy boundaries. We learn that we can change our agreed commitments or even change support people if we feel unsafe.

SHARE

I can say without a doubt that ACA saved my life, and it has definitely had its challenges. When I first came to ACA, my home group was made up of older white people. For a long time, I couldn't freely share about my experiences being a biracial Black and Filipino adult child. I felt unsafe facing the reality of my dysfunctional childhood messaging that was deeply rooted in racism, sexism, and homophobia in a room full of white people.

I was at a loss trying to find a sponsor in my home group, but I eventually found someone, thanks to the grace of my higher power. Although a white person, my sponsor is also queer, which is an identity I hold as well. I felt like I could share with them even if they didn't understand what it's like to be racially marginalized because they could empathize with the experience of being oppressed. I'm grateful we could have that understanding, so that my inner child and I felt safe with someone to walk the steps.

Find our own Inner Loving Parent and Reparent Our Inner Children

We use the language of a loving parent in sharing our recovery. Whoever is supporting us models the voice of an inner loving parent, which helps us find our own loving inner parent, to reparent our wounded inner child.

SHARE

I had ... therapists in the past. They were helpful, but the fact that my sponsor was willing to spend time week after week with me from the generosity of his heart helped me realize that I was worth it. He was a mirror for my own worth when I could not see it. Love was very transactional in my family. My sponsor loves me without wanting something back from me.

Build Self-Esteem

Our self-esteem increases as we learn that we did not make a mistake as children and we had nothing as children to be ashamed of. When we are supporting another, we realize that we can share our gifts and talents. We see that we can help another without giving advice, becoming judgmental, or acting as an authority figure.

SHARE

I haven't had a relationship in my life where someone just wanted to be there with no strings attached. It feels scary to write that, my brain immediately goes to places such as, should I give back to my sponsor? Do I deserve this relationship? But yes, yes, I do. I deserve a sponsor who cares about me, and I deserve to have people in my life who want to be there. I don't have to give to someone to know that they won't leave or abandon me because who I am is enough. Having a sponsor is helping me learn my own worth.

🌹 Meditation

Higher power, grant me the courage to take a blameless inventory of my childhood, the wisdom to tell the truth to a supporter, and the conviction to know that healing will result.

Learn to Support Others

As we grow in recovery, supporters help us develop a network of ACAs. They encourage us to offer help to them, too. At first, it may be offering a phone number or going out for coffee. As we progress, we will realize we have wisdom from working our program that we can extend to others. It may take time, but we see ourselves and others grow into our authentic selves.

SHARE

One of the most rewarding experiences was watching the faces of recovery. Frowns and stiffness softened into laughter and humility. I knew I was in a great recovery group when I witnessed others heal. Healthy boundaries replaced walls, higher powers replaced fears, feelings replaced numbness. It's hard work, transformation takes time, it's endless hours of writing and digging up buried feelings, as well as facing frustrating emotional blocks. Structure and discipline are key to our group's success.

See the Promises Come True

Supporters offer us a fresh perspective. As we work our program, we find those affirmations that work best for us to give us hope and reclaim the person our higher power intended us to be. (See Appendix B for a list of affirmations.) We read the Promises as possible for us! We learn to set boundaries, choose healthy people for relationships, play and have fun, and slowly release our dysfunctional behaviors. We enjoy feeling stable, peaceful, and financially secure.

SHARE

Towards the end of our time together, we both commented that the other person had changed, even if we couldn't see it for ourselves at the time. After we finished, I saw some of the changes benefiting my life.

SHARE

In Russia we have many channels at Telegram (one of the popular messenger apps) that help to recover. The channels appeared after the pandemic and increased in numbers over time. There are channels with online regular meetings, channels of the groups with in-person meetings where all information regarding a group is posted, and channels for supporting recovery. I believe the channels play an important role in connecting many people from different places across the country, who moved and live abroad, and even including people from former Soviet Union countries. Since the territory of our country is huge, some people who have no access to in-person meetings, for example, in towns and villages, and can reach the program only through these channels.

Some people are lucky to find sponsors in a short period. Others are not. Once I read the message of a girl who had a list of qualities for a sponsor and could find none. She asked if these qualities were enough to find a good sponsor. I shared that I had no list at all and prayed to higher power to send me a sponsor for recovery. It happened and my sponsor is the best for me in helping throughout my journey of overcoming the effects of being raised in an alcoholic family.

Some people request and share their experiences with sponsees, the issues they have to deal with, and how to solve them. In most cases, the solutions are wise and very helpful.

The second channel is Questions and Answers about ACA. I remind myself that having an open mind and open heart to new ideas and someone's experience could bring positive changes in my life, especially when so many program folks contribute.

One of the challenges is some people might behave in dysfunctional ways. Once I called a fellow traveler with a request for support in dealing with certain feelings. I was blamed for reaching step 10 and having no idea how to live through feelings. I politely finished the conversation and marked this fellow traveler as "never interact" in order to keep myself and my inner child protected. Fortunately, this kind of situation happens rarely. Most of the time, I am grateful for support I get and happy if my experience is of any help to others.

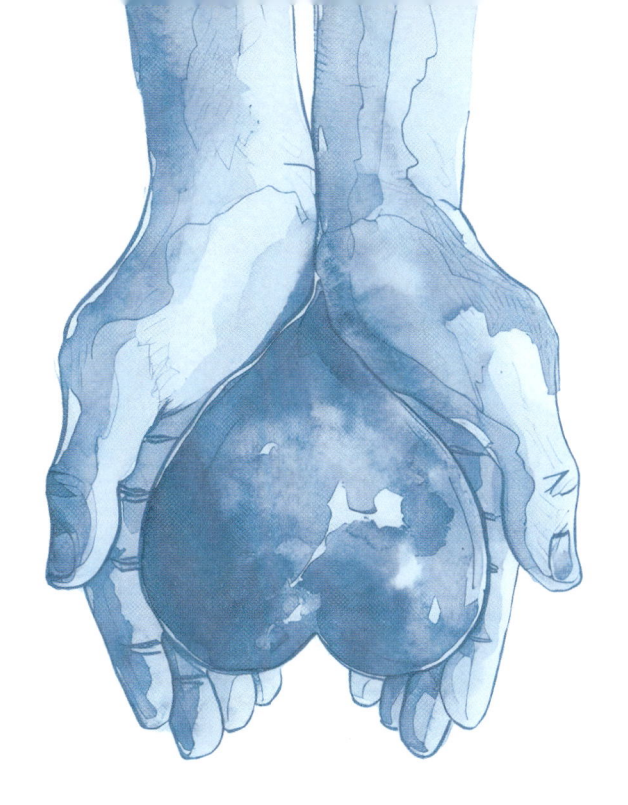

CHAPTER 4
GETTING STARTED WITH SUPPORT

THIS CHAPTER APPLIES to anyone looking for support, whether you are seeking a sponsor or someone to share with back and forth, such as a fellow traveler.

SHARE

As a person of color raised in a white family, it's hard to know where I fit in. I have fellow travelers who are white and fellow travelers who are BIPOC, and they each offer me a different opportunity to explore parts of myself and my conditioning. I didn't have many intimate relationships with people of color before coming to ACA, and I am so thankful for the safety to explore issues of racial trauma and internalized racism with ACA's who understand.

We look for supporters who have strong recovery and a willingness to share. This is often a trial-and-error process. Some of us look for people who have a similar life experience. Then, we may discover that it is less important than we thought. Some of us look for someone older or with more years in program and then find the perfect person sitting next to us in a beginners meeting.

SHARE

At our last in-person World Convention in Malmo, Sweden, we were asked to put a green dot on our clothing if we were willing to be a sponsor and a red one if we were looking for a sponsor. What a brilliant idea! I didn't need to think hard about it—I just stuck a green dot on my shirt. That green dot gave permission to my sponsee to approach me. We have been working on Zoom for four years—she in Russia, and I in the U.S.

We offer some ideas below, but caution that building healthy support networks requires being open-minded and willing to experiment. Chapter 11 of the *Big Red Book* contains useful information about qualities to look for or avoid in a sponsor relationship.

To be effective, a supporter should:

- Be active in their own recovery and have their own support network.
- Lead by example. They show up at meetings regularly and provide leadership and service at meetings.
- Honor commitments, deal with problems promptly, and are considerate and respectful of others.
- Speak lovingly and kindly, modeling the voice of an inner loving parent.
- Keep the focus on their ACA program.
- Practice strong boundaries.

SHARE

Part of the allure of ACA is that it doesn't tell me an exact formula to follow. It just provides enough guidance and support to become empowered over my life. Instead of someone else setting the rules of the road, I get to be the decider-in-chief of my recovery and my life. It breaks the spell of authority figures. It helps me find my internal compass and avoid referring to others to be okay. I have agency over my life. I answer to no one except my higher power, who I've come to believe through ACA deeply loves me unconditionally. Yet, I respect my higher power for his/her infinite power and wisdom. I use my higher power as my ultimate healing guide.

Experience has shown that we should avoid potential supporters who:
- Are active in any type of addiction.
- Ask to be your therapist or act like a therapist.
- Are overly directive, try to manage your life, or give unsolicited advice.
- Offer or ask for money, clothing, shelter, or a job.
- Try to become personally intimate or make sexual or romantic advances toward us.
- Feel unsafe.

SHARE

My sponsor told me he wanted to watch me grooming! This did not feel right to me.

Sometimes, it is difficult to recognize abusive or inappropriate behaviors. More information and resources are available in the safety tent card called "Preventing Unsafe Behavior in ACA." (See Appendix J). It references a special edition of ACA ComLine newsletter published March 2019 called, "Why We Need to Talk About Predatory Behavior."

Gender and/or Sexual Orientation:

Although there is no rule about working one-to-one with a supporter of the same gender or sexual orientation, it's advisable to pick a person with whom we are not likely to develop romantic feelings or sexual attraction, especially early in recovery. It can distract and complicate recovery for both parties. If it turns into an attraction, then it's advisable to find a supporter who will focus on recovery.

A person of the same gender identity may relate more directly to what it's like to grow up with that gender identity, not only in a dysfunctional home but in a dysfunctional culture. Issues with addiction and compulsive behaviors can have nuances shaped by gender identity. Sharing intimate details about our relationships and any sexual abuse may be easier with someone who shares a similar reality.

On the other hand, some of us have difficulty trusting those whose gender identity is the same as ours due to a history of abuse, neglect, or abandonment.

SHARE

My difficulty in finding a sponsor was compounded by the fact that I thought I needed to have a male sponsor (I am a man). My father was the alcoholic in my family, and so it was very hard for me to trust a male figure. When trying to find a sponsor, I thought about the 5th step and felt there were so many things I was afraid of revealing and/or discovering about myself. I kept asking myself, "Would I feel comfortable sharing [insert big scary thing that I have never shared with anyone]."

I also felt like I might discover new things about my gender and sexuality while going through the steps, and felt like I needed to find a sponsor who would be open and informed about these types of issues. I had experience being sponsored by two different men successively, before finding my current sponsor, who is a woman.

How to Find Supporters

When we want to work with another person on our recovery journey, we identify somebody we would like to work with, and then ask if they would be able to help us. How we go about this will be different depending on how long we have been in ACA or what type of relationship we are looking for. We recommend reading the section in chapter 11 of the *Big Red Book* about finding sponsors, much of which applies to all supporters.

When we're new to ACA recovery, we may seek out the familiar—someone who unconsciously reminds us of a parent or caretaker—or reflects our inner critical parent. Being alert to this possibility can help us pay attention to how we feel around someone. Do we leave those interactions feeling comfortable or uncomfortable? Are our needs met or unmet? Is our feeling based on the past or what we imagine the person might be thinking about us? We can use our internal feedback to help us choose with whom to work or readjust as needed.

SHARE

When I first came to ACA, I was defensive and fearful and easily triggered. Although I wouldn't have been able to identify it at the time, I was carrying around heaps of shame. My inner critical parent was in charge, a loud voice in my head that talked me out of my feelings and needs sometimes before I was even able to recognize them. ... How could I find the courage to ask someone to be my sponsor? Why would anyone agree to help me? I didn't deserve it.

And even if I did find the courage to ask, what then? My experience with "helpful people" had always seemed to include some sort of manipulation and unspoken agreement in which accepting their help meant that I forfeited my choices and power. I was terrified.

But somehow, despite all the fear that was blocking the way, my higher power guided me to a new way of doing things. That's the only way I can explain the fact that despite my misgivings, I found the courage to send an email to someone whose shares had really resonated with me.

Following are some suggestions about finding supporters:

Use the Meetings
- Some ACA meetings include a section calling for people who are available to support others to make themselves known, and to encourage those seeking support to ask somebody to work with them. If your meeting does not include this feature, attend a business meeting and suggest it. (See Appendix C for sample language.)
- Some people say during their sharing time at meetings that they are looking for support and ask for anybody who is interested to speak to them. We can approach a fellow ACA after listening to them sharing their story, and ask a question or ask for a phone number.
- The http://adultchildren.org website lists meetings that take place on the telephone and internet. These meetings frequently stay open for fellowship after the meeting ends and encourage people to state if they are looking for a sponsor.

Join a Study Group.
- We might find or be invited to join a study group, where we may choose to ask a member of the group to support us. Study groups that operate as meetings are listed under "meetings" at http://adultchildren.org. *A New Hope* and the *Ready, Set, Go!!* programs are designed for newcomers and are a good way to meet others in recovery.

Connections

Find Supporters at an Event
- Groups, intergroups, and regions frequently sponsor recovery events, which are often available online as well as in person. ACA holds an Annual World Convention, which since 2020 has been held online. Check http://acawso.org/worldconvention. You can often connect with people at these events if they are held on Zoom through the chat function.

SHARE

Things changed when I left my city to attend an ACA conference in another city, where ACA was more active and where there were going to be hundreds of attendees. I was going there specifically in hopes of finding a sponsor. I had a strong desire to progress in my recovery and had been praying and longing to find someone I would feel comfortable working with.

At this conference there was a panel discussion on sponsorship, and one of the questions discussed was on sponsorship and gender. That was where I realized that my sponsor didn't have to be a man at all. I also realized that my ssponsor did not have to be in the same city as me. My prayers were answered. I really identified specifically with one of the speakers at this conference, and went outside of my comfort zone to talk to that person afterwards, and asked them for their number. This person would turn out to become my sponsor.

Intergroups and regions meet regularly. You can attend your intergroup or region, volunteer for service, or simply observe and meet other ACAs who are active in service.

Consider offering service. Experienced ACA members are involved in offering service. You're likely to meet people who are dedicated to recovery at such events.

First Conversation, Establishing "Terms of Recovery Work"

When we find potential supporters, we talk to each other to establish how we would like the new relationship to work. This may change over time, but there are several areas to discuss in the beginning to establish how we will engage with each other. Doing so also gives us an opportunity to begin practicing healthy communication.

SHARE

I created a sponsorship agreement. I use this when I've been asked to sponsor someone. It helps me clarify my purpose as a sponsor and it helps set the sponsee's expectations. In that way, we both can be accountable to one another. My sponsorship agreement clearly encapsulates my boundaries for best ensuring a fruitful healing process for both of us.

See Appendix D for one member's sponsorship agreement.

Here are some helpful questions for starting a support relationship:

- What is the primary program work we will focus on: step work, reparenting, feelings work, grief work, laundry list trait work. Which type of work feels the most pressing?
- Is there any type of work I am not ready for yet?
- Are there any potential challenges or barriers in working together?
- What brought me to ACA? (To uncover what motivates us to work an ACA program.)
- What changes am I hoping for in working with a supporting person or a group?

- What are my goals and boundaries, expectations, and commitments?
- Do I have any fears?
- What is my prior experience with sponsorship or support? (however we define it)
- What process will we use to decide if we should end the support relationship?
- What are healthy communication ideas to try before ending the relationship abruptly? (Note: This does not apply in abusive / unethical situations.)
- How will we address possible changes in our relationship?
- Do we want to work together for a trial period to see how we work together?

SHARE

As a member of the LGBTQIA+ community, I have, over the last 5 years in the program, come to believe that the most crucial part of my recovery is to be validated and seen in the light of other non-monogamous LGBTQIA+ ACAs.

When I first entered ACA, I was in a desperate need of releasing the burden of unexpressed grief and grasped for every little connection and recovery tool that could ease my agony of feeling alone. I could feel the sadness of my inner children and the rage from my inner teenagers due to the carry-overs of homophobia and transphobia as some of the generational traumas.

When I was 15 years old, I sat with my maternal grandpa on his porch one evening. He was my best friend during my childhood, and I felt so excited to tell him about my new queer crush. His whole body language changed from love to disgust. He mumbled something homophobic about gay people and left me alone at the porch. In the shift of that moment, time just stopped. I felt the combination of contempt crawling under my skin with a feeling of just dissolving into invisible existence. From feeling belonging, to feeling invisible.

The dysfunctional rules "don't talk, don't trust, and don't feel" needs to be replaced with "talk, trust, and feel" to recover and for me, as a non-monogamous queer nonbinary person, I feel trust when I hear my sponsee share about her concerns with her girlfriend. I soften when I hear my fellow traveler share their joy about their wife meeting their new partner. I feel seen when my sponsor validates my queerness as I share about my relationships.

When I can see all the parts of myself in other ACA's, including my gender and sexuality, I heal the wounds of my inner children and inner teenagers and break the cycle of generational trauma.

CHAPTER 5
KEY COMMITMENTS IN SUPPORT RELATIONSHIPS

MOST OF THESE COMMITMENTS apply equally to the sharing person and the supporting person—whether in a meeting, small group, or working one-to-one. Some of these commitments may come earlier or later in the relationship.

These commitments address the process of supporting each other—the loving principles that guide our conversations. They are different from the goals of program work. We sometimes refer to them as the "tools" of recovery.

Commitments Around the Meeting Process

1. Respect each member's time and adhere to time agreements for working together.
2. Set schedule, goals, and accountability for progress in program.
3. Meet in person or by phone regularly or whatever structure is agreed upon.

SHARE

The sponsor I had was from Russia and went with me through the steps 1 to 3. She set boundaries with me from the beginning. For example, ... if I wouldn't follow through with arranged phone calls, she would drop me after the third time. I didn't hear much about her journey, but we started and ended the call with the feeling exercise. She asked me, after reading my part on the step work, very specific questions about things that had been coming up for her. Sometimes, that was quite irritating, but I did really appreciate her clarity and guidance.

Commitments About How We Share and Respond

Remember that the "sharing person" below may be a sponsee, a fellow traveler, or someone in group work. The supporting person may be a sponsor, a fellow traveler, or someone in group work who is in the role of listening and giving gentle guidance.

SHARE

As a sponsor, I resist the ACA trait of fixing and rescuing when I am asked for my advice about a problem. When I feel urgency to offer my opinion, I try to pause. I ask my sponsee what her inner child wants to say. Often, the child knows the answer before we do. Then I offer program tools—how can relying on spiritual resources such as patience, compassion, and love put the problem in perspective? My role is not to problem solve. It's to direct attention to our program tools.

The Supporting Person Agrees To:

1. Identify triggers and the voice of the sharing person's inner critical parent.
2. Mirror back the sharing person's voice so they can hear it.
3. Help the sharing person identify and share feelings.
4. Help the sharing person find their inner family, allow the inner children to speak, and show ways to "reparent" the inner child.
5. Help the sharing person find their "true self" by exploring longings, desires, etc.
6. Respond to questions and challenges based on literature and experience rather than personal opinions.
7. Identify denial when necessary.
8. Be honest, gentle, and kind.
9. Avoid being critical, controlling, or acting as an authority figure.
10. Identify, recognize, and acknowledge progress. Whether we call our progress in the ACA program goals, milestones, accomplishments, or celebrations, as we progress, our program work turns into action that marks change. Appendix E includes Key Recovery Goals/Milestones.
11. Encourage outreach by the sharing person to support others in their recovery. Agree on steps to take to help carry the message.

SHARE

My sponsor encouraged me to start being involved in service. From the AWC [ACA World Convention] online meeting, I found out about global opportunities and got involved in Global Service Volunteers on service committees and support sponsorship and 12 step study groups. My higher power has given me vision, purpose, and direction for my life, and I am passing it on to others with much gratefulness.

The Sharing Person Agrees To:
1. Keep commitments to meet and be prepared and communicate in advance if they cannot keep a meeting or program work date.
2. Be willing to change, i.e., be honest, open, and willing.

Both Parties Will:
1. Speak openly, honestly, and lovingly.

SHARE

When [my sponsor] was experiencing a lot of turmoil in her family and wasn't so available for a longer period of time, I hid my feeling of abandonment and pretended I was ok. I wasn't. It all came out in quiet resentment when we met online, and that was the last straw for her in her challenged place. I made my amends to myself and her. She had taught me to forgive myself first before even considering amending someone else, to make sure I can receive forgiveness for my actions.

2. Refrain from gossip or talking about each other to other people except with our express consent.
3. Honor anonymity and confidentiality, except as expressly agreed, i.e., if we agree we may discuss our relationship with our other supporters.
4. Say "I don't know" when we don't know.
5. Be candid about what is not working in the support relationship. Agree to regular checkpoints where we mutually assess what is working and not working.
6. Be willing to make changes in the relationship or end the relationship without guilt or shame.

SHARE

I have ACAs who want to work through the Yellow Workbook and want someone to guide them through it. A couple of them have reached a point in that book where they begin to struggle with one of the steps. Hearing their pain, I suggest we take a time out from that work for a bit.

We discuss options such as reading on a specific issue they seem to be having, like grief and/or self-nurture through self-parenting. Whatever their decision, I listen and remain flexible for them. I find that this type of relationship benefits both the person I am working with and me as well. While listening to the person I am working with, it often happens that I find clarity in an issue that I have been with, or I find issues that are yet unresolved within me.

Meditation

Grant me the courage to reach out with love to newcomers in recovery, the acceptance to know that I am good enough to offer help, and the wisdom to know that one ACA helping another is how recovery happens.

SHARE

I'm a member of other fellowships besides ACA. Hearing stories of others' experiences, I was lucky in AA. My sponsor and grand-sponsor in AA treated me with gentleness, kindness, respect, and compassion. When I got into ACA, I heard stories of others' experiences in those fellowships, which were not like my own. These people had experienced a lot of trauma, hierarchical relationships, and general disrespect. I was blessed in ACA to start with a fellow traveler who exemplified the same characteristics as my AA and other fellowship sponsors. The man exemplified compassion and respect.

Since then, I have had the opportunity to observe many fellow traveler relationships, and some of these fellow travelers have complained that their fellow traveler did not stick it out and complete the steps with them. What seems to work for those members of ACA is to ask for and work with a fellow traveler for a single step. A number of members have indicated that this has worked for them.

One concern is that we are all adult children at various stages of recovery. I can't expect my fellow travelers to be perfect, to not make mistakes, to not say and do things that hurt my feelings. One of the great opportunities that I have had in working with fellow travelers is to practice the art of forgiveness. That's not always easy. However, it's important for me to realize that I make mistakes, and I say things and do things that essentially are lapses in my recovery.

I don't like the term "relapse" in ACA. Relapse seems to indicate that I go back all the way back to the beginning. That's never been true for me, and I haven't seen it be true for anyone else. I do experience lapses, and there may be several in a day where, in that moment, my wounded inner child takes command or my loving parent takes a break, and the critical parent sees the void and comes back. I can get back on track by talking to others, whether I call them sponsor, sponsee, fellow, traveler, co-sponsor, or mentor.

CHAPTER 6
POTENTIAL CHALLENGES IN SUPPORT RELATIONSHIPS

THE FOLLOWING SECTION highlights some potential challenges we may encounter in support relationships. We offer some possible solutions. Above all else, we caution to remember that we are all adult children trying to do the best we can in helping each other.

These issues can arise in any support setting, including meetings, study groups, fellow travelers, and sponsor-sponsee relationships. We offer some common challenges and possible solutions:

Lack of Trust

Perhaps the greatest challenge in getting support from other people in ACA is lack of trust. We fear or feel suspicious or angry toward authority figures because we don't trust. Our caregivers did not consistently meet our core needs in childhood, so it's natural that we have difficulties trusting others. When we think about sharing our story and speaking honestly with another person, we may feel afraid or ashamed, or anticipate feeling uncomfortable. We may worry that our secrets will be divulged to others. Because we lack a sense of emotional safety, we may choose isolation over sharing our story. We fear we will ask someone and they will say "no."

SHARE

I'm a Filipina-American, whose racial sobriety was mostly intellectual until 2020, when PGM [People of the Global Majority] and anti-Asian murders necessitated its immediate deepening, at the gut and cellular level.

At the numerous new PGM meetings that started up in response, the shortage of sponsors of color was glaring. I was sponsoring two white women at the time. Accustomed to minimizing racism's impact, I had never thought about their race. But amid the collective trauma of ongoing racial violence, I committed to taking on two more—this time, sponsees of color.

I've since declined requests from the white recovery family. By systemic default, their access to sponsors with similar life experiences is plentiful. Reserving my emotional labor only for PGMs leaves me with a full heart and renewed racial wholeness. In this ongoing time of reckoning, I continue choosing to carry the message of ACA only to people who look like me.

🪷 Meditation

Higher power, help me to work with my supporters to develop trust and lose the fear of dislodging my "stuck grief," knowing that I can trust myself, my supporters, my program, and my higher power or spiritual connection.

As the laundry list traits show, most of us did not learn as children how to develop and maintain healthy relationships. The "don't tell" rule meant we didn't learn how to speak honestly. The "don't feel" rule meant we stuffed our feelings, bottled up shame, fear, and anger, which may emerge in adult relationships in unhealthy ways. The "don't trust" rule meant that we felt isolated and unable to form connections with others.

SHARE

Growing up in family dysfunction, one of my deepest wounds is trust. I was taught not to trust myself, and thus, I had nothing to gauge trust with others. Yet, I needed to come out of my emotional isolation and connect with others to heal in ACA recovery. Sponsorship didn't work for me, as my authority issues ran too deep. I'm grateful I've been able to connect with others deeply in ACA to rebuild trust outside the traditional sponsor/sponsee model.

As we come out of isolation and learn to speak about our past with our supporters, we may feel uncomfortable or afraid. We may unconsciously repeat patterns learned in childhood in our support relationships. This applies both to the sharing person and the supporting person. No matter how much experience we have in program, we can be triggered into childhood reactions.

Solution

Building trust takes time. We build trust by keeping commitments and genuinely listening to each other. We ask if the other party is open to feedback and avoid giving advice if they are not.

Slowly, we will begin to trust that our supporting person really does want to hear what we have to say. When we are heard without judgment, we begin to trust that healing is possible. When we feel uncomfortable, we can share our feelings honestly, and know we will not be judged. As we identify the voice of our inner critical parent and see that our supporting person does not criticize or berate us, we begin to trust that recovery is possible.

Either Party is Not Meeting Commitments

Abandonment is a key laundry list trait. When we commit to calling someone on the phone, showing up at a meeting, or participating in a group study, we recognize that honoring our commitments helps others in our network feel honored, respected, and heard. If we take on a service commitment, we honor the terms of the commitment or find a substitute if necessary. If we agree to meet one-to-one with a supporter, we respect the time and energy we both devote to these meetings and we both show up when we say we will.

If we become uncomfortable, feel unsafe, and want to change our commitments, we step back, seek discernment from our higher power or spiritual principles, and then seek a solution.

Solution

If issues of safety, time commitment, or boundaries arise in our support network, we practice honesty and clear communication, recognizing that we have the right to change our minds. First, we examine if our issue is one that calls for acceptance rather than action. We discuss our concerns with trusted advisers, being sure that we are acting, not reacting.

In one-to-one work with program materials, we may feel the need to change the original focus. For example, it may be that Step Work cannot proceed meaningfully until some feelings work takes place. It may be that family-of-origin work needs to be more in depth than step 4 requires. We check our motivations, recognizing that we may be able to work through our fears. We seek to avoid perfectionism and practice loving care for ourselves by agreeing with our supporters on a revised plan of program work.

Sometimes, we might not be ready for a step or other piece of recovery work and might need to return to a previous step or pause work and spend more time attending meetings, especially speaker meetings, to help identify as an adult child. A supporter might suggest taking more space, allowing the other person to be in touch when they're ready to resume.

SHARE

I almost stopped going about 6 months into my journey because I felt like I did not connect. I was fortunate that I knew from experience that I should continue and complete my goal of working the steps in ACA, regardless of my inner dialogue. It was highly suggested that I get a sponsor and a therapist. Initially, I was reluctant, but then identified that my reluctance may be disease/trauma based. ... I have realized that a large part of my inner healing is created when I "trust the process."

By regularly "checking in" with each other, we become aware when the commitments made on the original plan are not yielding progress in program. As the ultimate goal of all recovery work is to reclaim our authentic selves, we can practice being authentic by talking about the program we have agreed to. What is working well? What is not? What can we decide to do or change?

SHARE

After our first 30 days of working together, I send [the person] an email to check in to see how it's going. I do it via email in case they're scared to tell me that they don't want to continue working with me, or something else that's difficult for them. I also take this opportunity myself to check in to see if I want to continue working with that person. I do the same thing at the 90-day point. After that, I let the sponsee know that it's up to them to bring up any difficulties they might have in working with me.

For group work, all parties generally commit to attend meetings and do any required homework. Where such commitments are not being met, the group may, by group conscience, decide what action to take.

Differences in Working Pace or Style

As adult children who have lost our identities as children, it can be hard to know what we need in a support relationship. It can take time for us to understand and attune to our needs. In one-to-one program work, either party may become uncomfortable with the pace of program work and/or the working style of the supporters.

Solution

When we judge our recovery efforts as "too slow," we can remember our willingness and give ourselves credit for the work we are doing. We all have a different pace.

In one-to-one support relationships, we may want to move at a slower pace than initially agreed. This is an opportunity to practice healthy communication and state what we need.

Pace can also be affected by the internal parts of us that resist recovery work. Our supporter can help us by asking questions and supporting us to understand our resistance.

When we are new, we may want to move quickly to get through the work to feel self-esteem or to get the benefits of recovery. As we progress, we realize that recovery is not a race. We will probably want to work program materials multiple times. We check our motivations, sometimes realizing that our recovery work is proceeding just as it should.

Perhaps we want to change meetings to focus on a particular type of work. Where possible, we honor the time commitment to a group study, recognizing that the group depends on unity and trust among members.

We must beware of the false thinking of "this is not the right supporter; someone else would be better." This may be our perfectionism arising, or it may be resistance to the pain of program work. We realize that our supporters are not the inner critical parent. They genuinely desire recovery for us and them. We can both practice healthy relationship behaviors by working through resistance using program tools.

SHARE

Sometimes, a member of a support relationship may leave the program. If this happens, we have compassion but do not overly invest in someone staying in the program or try to chase them down. We avoid rescuing or enabling, both of which are codependent behaviors. Each person's path is unique and we respect their autonomy.

Feeling Uncomfortable and/or Unsafe

As adult children, we may experience triggers that remind us of the lack of safety we felt in childhood. These triggers may initially appear as discomfort. Perhaps our families lacked boundaries. Perhaps they kept secrets and enlisted us in that sickness. Perhaps they said one thing, but did another. Maybe we were not listened to, or our opinions were discounted. These triggers can arise in any support setting, from meetings to one-to-one support.

There may be times when we start to feel a support relationship does not feel right. We may start to feel isolated from other fellow travelers, spending too much time with one supporter.

Occasionally, we may feel our supporter is too interested in our daily life and relationships. They may start giving gifts and showing up unexpectedly where we are. We may start receiving too many texts, which may feel even subtly suggestive.

Solution

It may be appropriate to talk confidentially with a more experienced ACA about what is happening to seek out an objective perspective and possibly develop some healthy strategies moving forward. We may also want to check out the ACA Safety Tent Card. (See Appendix J)

In talking with those we trust, we may come to see that our safety issue is a trigger from the past. Perhaps another person's personality or physical demeanor reminds us of our childhood. It's ok. If this feeling doesn't seem to lessen, we can set a boundary with that supporter. We can take care of ourselves.

If we feel uncomfortable or unsafe with any person, we can ask for help. We can discuss the issue with our supporters or raise the issue at a business meeting. We assess whether fear of authority or people-pleasing may be keeping us from standing up for ourselves. Confronting lack of safety is one of the hardest issues to handle in recovery, but there are those who know how we feel.

SHARE

When we finished the 12 steps, we moved on to the Laundry Lists Workbook, and things fell apart in our group. One member started attacking others in our area via email and text (preying on those who were still stuck in the dysfunction) and metaphorically lobbing bombs at others individually and in meetings. She left the LL group and the meeting she attended opted to read the ACA booklet "Good Enough Group," which helped us all reaffirm that our meeting group is more powerful than one individual, and unlike our families of origin, our meeting group "circled the wagons" to protect the group ... I share all that to illustrate that even though some very intense healing and growth happens, sometimes it's not enough. Personally, I grew tremendously from both of those experiences. I stayed connected to my HP, to my fellows and I didn't abandon myself through it all.

The Supporting Person May Appear as an Authority Figure or Fixer

As with the section above, we can ask if this appearance is genuine or a trigger from the past. In any support setting where the parties share back and forth, either party can appear to be offering unwanted advice, becoming judgmental, or otherwise appearing as an authority.

SHARE

My main take away is that sponsors don't work well. There is just too much temptation to control others. I know I'm extremely sensitive to any work or reaction that is controlling. I have had it happen all my life. Several members in the region that I know had that issue with a sponsor. I like the fellow traveler model. With mine, this was the first relationship where I felt I was equal. I didn't owe him anything, and if he was busy or didn't have time, that was fine. For me, the local group was too small, and I know in Thailand, gossip gets around quickly. So for me, I wanted a fellow traveler located outside the country with no risk of any interaction with my local community. The ironic thing is that even though my fellow traveler lives in Australia, it still is a small online ecommunity, so he knows many of the members I know, and the same for him.

When working through the steps and the traits, I had huge breakthroughs and made good progress. It is when I actually could make personality changes, specifically my bad temper.

Solution

Sometimes, simply pointing out that we feel uncomfortable is enough for the other person to apologize and set things straight. We realize that no one wants to act out the laundry list characteristics when helping another.

Sometimes, we may misunderstand something that has been said in a helpful spirit. After all, we are human. Another person may share their experience, strength, and hope in a way that sounds to us like we "should do" the same thing. We remember that we are all free to make our own choices and that exercising choice is part of recovery.

SHARE

I've learned that I can't sponsor someone who seems to want me to fix them and doesn't take program actions. It's too close to my core wound of being a parentified hero child of a mother who never left an abusive situation. I no longer push myself into thinking I "should" be able to work with everyone. I might get there someday, but I'm not there yet. For now, it works best for me to sponsor people who are willing to do whatever it takes to recover. That's what worked for me in my recovery, so that's the experience I have to share.

Either Party May Fall into People-Pleasing.

Sometimes, in an effort to achieve an intimate relationship, either party in a support relationship may fall into people-pleasing, agreeing with the other when they aren't clear about what is being said or failing to be honest about what they don't understand.

Solution

We remember we may be using people-pleasing as a strategy to avoid criticism. We are working our program to balance or release these traits. With loving support from our higher power or our spiritual principles, we recognize when we fall into people-pleasing and seek to be our authentic selves.

Meditation

Higher power, may I have the strength to remain steadfast when recovery feels difficult, the courage to confront difficulties with the help of a fellow traveler, and the wisdom to know that healing will result.

SHARE

My first ACA meeting was a small, Georgia-based Zoom meeting. The newcomer honeymoon feelings shortly wore off as I attempted vulnerability in a room full of mostly white faces. I felt a need to represent my community in a way that did not reinforce negative stereotypes about us. I felt I had more to lose sharing about my parents struggling with addiction while trying to raise us as traumatized, underemployed, and underearning first-generation Americans.

I found a fellow traveler in this group, and we worked through the Yellow Workbook as co-sponsors. Things changed around step 4. Her reactions to my shares included "Oh wow," and "That's crazy." Though I knew we were both ACA, I felt separated into my own category of "messed up" ascribed only to black and brown people. This experience of feeling othered is all too common in my exchanges with white people.

When I shared this with her, she apologized profusely—my first practice of emotional sobriety. Taking the time to educate her on why that seemingly innocuous comment was offensive required a lot of emotional labor. I stopped working with her shortly after and continued my recovery with a sponsor I met in a PGM [People of the Global Majority] meeting. I still attend meetings of all heritages, but as a queer, Jamaican- and Dominican-American, I feel the most comfortable in PGM-designated spaces.

CHAPTER 7
FOR SPONSORS OR THOSE CONSIDERING SPONSORSHIP

THE WSO WEBSITE defines a sponsor as follows: "A sponsor is someone who attends ACA meetings regularly and who has worked the ACA 12 steps. The person has made progress in recovering from the effects of growing up in a dysfunctional home." The sponsor, unlike all the other support relationships discussed in this Guide, supports a sponsee by keeping the focus on the sponsee, and sharing their own experience only when helpful to the sponsee's recovery. Some ACAs resist when asked by someone to become a "sponsor." They may feel that the level of experience and the responsibility of guiding another's recovery program is overwhelming.

SHARE

The greatest portion of my healing and recovery in ACA came from doing the ACA 12 steps. The next most important thing I've ever done for my recovery is to become a sponsor. I get so much out of sponsoring; it's really incredible how many insights into my own recovery come from working with sponsees! It strengthens my recovery like nothing else!

Although many in ACA prefer to work with a fellow traveler, recovery partner, or co-sponsor in their recovery and choose not to seek a sponsor, we know that many newcomers want to find a sponsor. We also recognize that there are fewer people willing to sponsor than needed. This section is particularly directed to the ACA who is asked to be a sponsor and questions if they are ready or able to sponsor.

Challenges in Becoming Willing to Sponsor

The primary challenges to being willing to support another or offering to support another fall into the main categories discussed below:

I'm Not Ready

Many of us may feel that a sponsor must have substantial years in recovery or must have worked the steps and done other program work before being ready to support another person. We may feel inadequate to help another person face their pain or offer solutions for recovery. We often fail to see that our "I'm not ready" reaction may be a trigger to one of our laundry list traits.

Solution

Perhaps we are ready to shed the laundry list trait telling us we are not good enough and make a commitment to our self-worth. We must remember that a sponsor in ACA differs from a "sponsor" in some other 12 step recovery groups. ACA sponsorship is distinguished from other 12 step programs in that the sponsor is not someone who tries to "manage someone else's life," but uses a more gentle, non-directive approach.

We do not give orders or directions or threaten to leave a sponsee because of where they are in their recovery program. We learn to listen, which is a gift of immeasurable value. We learn patience and nurturing, things we did not learn as children. We affirm to the sponsee that we are all equal and deserving of recovery.

If we find ourselves responding that there are other people more qualified than we are to offer support, we pause and ask our higher power if this concern should keep us from offering support. The other person asked us for a reason. Surely, they saw something in us that offered hope for recovery.

We believe being a compassionate listener is the most important qualification. We all can be compassionate listeners regardless of our length in program.

SHARE

I've been blessed with substantial relief from my adult child ways. As such, I have experiences I'm willing to share with others in humility. I know my answers are not my sponsee's answers to what vexes them. But I can be a cheerleader in encouraging their process. I can be a witness when no one else was there to see what was happening. I can be compassionate and empathetic because I have healed. I can model sobriety while experiencing a whole palette full of emotions for my sponsees to see.

Fear of Intimacy, Divulging Secrets, or Not Being Liked.
When we arrive at ACA, many of us are isolated and afraid that others will not like us. This trait can keep us from offering support.

Solution
We know that isolation is not healthy. We realize that our recovery depends upon making healthy connections with other people. Offering support is one way to practice this. Most people who offer to be a sponsor also have their own support network. We carry shame from our past

and are weighed down by the family secrets we have kept. Even after some time in program, some of us find our reaction to being asked to sponsor triggers these childhood fears. As we work through this reaction with our own supporters, we come to see that we have much in common with the newcomer. This helps us see that our experience can help us overcome these fears. We reassure the sponsee that what they say is confidential. We will not reveal their secrets. We tell the truth with love.

SHARE

An ACA sponsor (or a support person) does many things: They help us apply the program to our daily lives, but they also help us learn to trust. When I entered ACA. I dreaded being judged. My early ACA sponsors taught me I could be completely vulnerable.

Today, I can speak my doubts and double-check my thinking. When I share my problems, they are solved with grace. I thank ACA for many gifts, but the chance to share my life with a sponsor and the chance to support others as their sponsor is one of the greatest. I am no longer alone. To me, that gift is priceless.

Fear of Becoming an Authority Figure or Fixer/Rescuer
We may have had an experience with support in another program where a sponsor triggered our fear of authority figures or gave us unwanted advice. Friends and family may have also been advice-givers. These triggers may keep us from offering to sponsor.

Solution
We can state our concerns honestly and ask to be gently reminded if the sponsee begins to feel that we are acting as an authority, fixer, or rescuer. We remember that recovery is a process. We appreciate our ability to work on these laundry list traits ourselves in recovery work.

SHARE

At first, I was hesitant. I didn't want to fall into a trap of rescuing, being codependent, or worse, be seen as superior, arrogant, or an authority figure. I decided to try with the condition that I could only be myself and share what I know to be true for me, and that may not be true for them. We had clear expectations that I wasn't going to be any of the above types described. I could only give away what I had, and it was up to them to see if it had any value, and it was ok if it didn't.

Fear of Commitment

We fear commitment. What if it doesn't work out? What if the sponsee wants to quit? We know from working our own program that fear of commitment holds us back in developing healthy relationships.

Solution

We jointly agree on how we will work together and then make a commitment to follow through on our agreements. By practicing recovery work, our fear of commitment lessens. We see that the sponsee has also made a commitment to us.

We accept that we are not in charge of anyone's recovery. People may leave the program. Our role is to support, not to control.

SHARE

My sister traveler and I had met a couple of times for meals and swimming with her heart child when we happened to be visiting the others' town. I had enjoyed the growing friendship and our shared witchy and queer-feminist values. Now I felt that I might have abused my power as a sponsor and sponsoring where I have the power of experience, to meet my unmet social needs, my need for friends, in the same way my father used his emotional power to cover up a lack of connection and feeling socially inferior.

I reached out to my relationship sponsor. To my big surprise and relief, she didn't see that I had overstepped any boundaries. My inner fear of being just like my father, the shame of my loneliness, and comparison to younger people more socially connected than me had covered up the reality of the situation that was more balanced. I would never have realized that on my own.

We Think We Don't Have Time

Sometimes, we tell ourselves that we are too busy to be a sponsor. How do we balance sponsoring with our own recovery program and life obligations?

Solution

We are realistic about our time constraints but cautious when we believe that we may be making excuses to stay isolated or protect ourselves. We remember how much time we put into codependence and caretaking of others, time that can now be used to support the recovery of another. We welcome sponsees into our lives, knowing they may grow to be part of our recovery network.

SHARE

When I finished the steps, my sponsor told me that she would be available to me until the end of her life, and that's how it is for me and my sponsees. It's a true gift to have someone in my life who has followed my ACA journey from the beginning and who knows me well. She helps me with my blind spots. I try to do the same for my sponsees.

We can put limits on the time we will sponsor another by being a temporary sponsor, or we may agree to sponsor for a limited purpose, for example, to hear a 4th step.

When Am I Ready to Become a Sponsor?

Agreeing to sponsor can be daunting, but we can consider doing so at certain times in our journey. The following are important moments when we might consider becoming a sponsor.

- When I am ready to share my recovery experience with Step Work, Reparenting, Feeling or Grief Work, and/or Trait Work. "Progress, not perfection."
- When I have established a relationship with another newcomer.
- When someone asks me.
- When my supporters ask me to consider it.
- When my higher power tells me I am ready.
- When I have a support network that can help me if I have questions or concerns.

SHARE

We met in AA and had discussed ACA briefly. I let her know when she was interested in doing any work, I would be available. Within the year, in a small group, we began to meet once a week at a fellow traveler's home to read and share. After four months, she had many questions, and a fellow traveler recommended a sponsor would be a helpful guide.

She turned to me and asked if I would be her sponsor. Without hesitation, I said, "yes." We made a date to get together. I told her we would spend some time sharing our stories, getting to know each other, and we would choose how to move forward from there.

In my six years of ACA, I'd preferred the fellow traveler model, so I felt nervous to be a sponsor. I read up on sponsorship, I prayed, I reached out to trusted fellow travelers, and I came to the conclusion I've been "working it" and making progress. I've got a lot to share.

I had experience as an Al-Anon and AA sponsor, but my instincts were telling me an ACA sponsor [would] be far different. Right before our first visit, I checked in with my inner family, read The Solution, let go of my perfectionism, said the Serenity prayer, breathed some gentle breaths, and had my ACA literature by my side. I felt ready to connect to another adult child. She had expectations of going through work as done in AA and was very overwhelmed. I continued to remind her that she wasn't alone, and we would always take it at a pace that felt the best for her. I talked her through the ACA Sponsorship:Fellow Travelers [chapter in the Big Red Book]and reviewed the inner family. I let our conversation guide what we read in the Big Red Book.

I continue to encourage her to plan for recovery, do a nightly inventory with compassion, take gentleness breaks, connect to her higher power, practice the ACA serenity prayer, stay in touch with fellow travelers, keep coming back, because you're worth it and together we can do something wonderful!

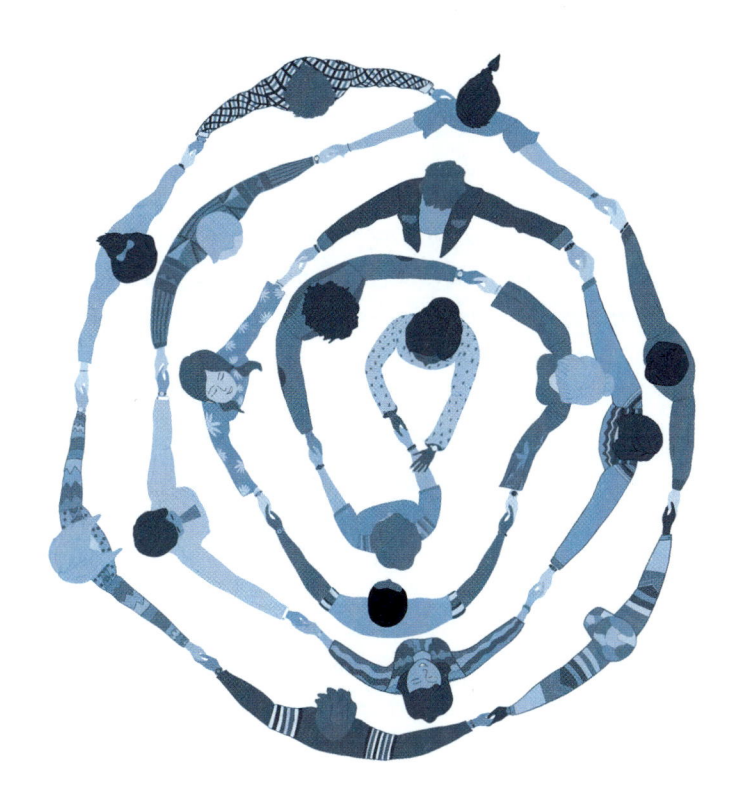

CHAPTER 8
CONCLUSION

RECOVERY INVOLVES COMING OUT of isolation and learning to build healthy relationships with other people, which most of us did not learn as children. We learn how to ask for help and accept it. Helping and supporting others is an integral part of the ACA healing process. We learn to talk, trust, feel, and remember.

SHARE

I am a dark-complexioned son of refugee immigrants from the Dominican Republic born in The Bronx in the early 60s. Alcoholism stunted my father's emotional growth, and he abandoned the family when I was very young. Mom's lack of self-esteem impoverished my soul.

Connections

> *I "discovered" ACA in my mid-20s and found a fellowship that offered unconditional support. Yes, there were hints of classism or racism, but the overwhelming sense was that we were all in the same "boat."*
>
> *In ACA, I have worked with whites, blacks, Asians, and Latinos; male and females; straight and gay; Jews, Muslims, and gentiles, young and old.*

The idea that anyone walking into an ACA meeting isn't welcomed with an open heart is contrary to our own best interest. Welcoming a new member of any persuasion opens our hearts to healing those aspects of ourselves that we do not know about or like.

Everyone will create their own path to recovery and healing. ACA does not offer one "right" recovery plan for all people at all times. The nature of our recovery may evolve as we change and grow in our program. Also, regardless of the terms used, the benefits, commitments, and problems that may arise are common for us all.

Remember: We do not have to recover alone. Recovery is a process and takes time and patience. As we work our program together with our supporters, we will learn to expect the best and get it!

APPENDIX A—
2017 BALLOT PROPOSAL 2017-4

The following proposal was passed at the wso Annual Business Conference:

We propose that the wso revise BRB chapter 11 and the sponsorship pamphlet for clarity and consistency. The word "sponsor" is used throughout the chapter and elsewhere in the BRB. However, under direct sponsorship, instead of "sponsor," the word "fellow traveler" is used. This leads to confusion. We believe you recommend that all sponsors follow the fellow traveler method, meaning both are on equal footing. This method tries to prevent the sponsee from becoming triggered in believing the sponsor is an authority figure.

We recommend:

1. Defining, at the chapter start, that anyone on the ACA path of recovery, regardless of their time and progress in the program, is a fellow traveler.

2. Defining, at the chapter start, that not all fellow travelers can be sponsors, as per the requirements outlined in the BRB. (See #3.)

3. Changing "fellow traveler" to "sponsor" under the heading "Direct sponsorship."

4. Clarifying that the "fellow traveler" method supports a relationship in which sponsor and sponsee are on equal footing, rather than in teacher-student roles.

    Clarify the requirements of a sponsor (the type referred to as "traditional" in the pamphlet and "fellow traveler in BRB). From the wso website: "A sponsor is someone who attends ACA meetings regularly and who has worked the ACA 12 steps. The person has made progress in recovering from the effects of growing up in a dysfunctional home." Not all fellow travelers meet this requirement. We need clarification in chapter 11 about this and consistency between the website and pamphlet.

5. Adding that one of the supports a sponsor provides is to help the sponsee connect with their loving parent and inner child.

> Clarifying the terms fellow traveler and sponsor would support both sponsors and sponsees to be on the same page and reduce confusion. Our group encourages members to contact fellow travelers who can be there if they don't have a sponsor, when their sponsor is unavailable and in addition to their sponsor.

APPENDIX B—AFFIRMATIONS FOR THOSE IN SUPPORT RELATIONSHIPS

I am worthy of sharing and obtaining recovery.

I rely on a higher power or spiritual principles as the ultimate authority in recovery.

I ask for support without feeling like I am a burden.

I define who I am. I am good, and I accept only what is good and healthy in my life.

I will treat others with respect and expect others to treat me with respect.

I can be equal in a relationship with another person who has more or less experience than me.

I am capable of selecting healthy support people.

I am willing to do whatever it takes to recover.

I can say, "I do not understand," or "Please explain again" if I am confused.

I can say, "Please Slow Down" if I feel overwhelmed.

A support person can be my ally, but only I can do my work.

I work the ACA program according to my current ability: It doesn't have to be perfect to be worthwhile.

I share my experience rather than giving advice, fixing, or rescuing.

I choose to be isolated no longer.

I trust myself.

I am gentle with myself.

I listen to and treat my inner child with gentleness, kindness, love, and respect.

I allow myself to dream and have hope.

APPENDIX C—SAMPLE MEETING LANGUAGE ABOUT FINDING SUPPORTERS

Here is some suggested language to be used in meetings to encourage asking for and offering support.

Part of this program is coming out of isolation and connecting with others. There are several ways you can do this:

- Fellow Travelers, Co-sponsors, or Recovery Partners are two or more people who work through the ACA program together, sharing and supporting each other's recovery back and forth.
- A step group is a group of people who work the 12 steps together.
- A sponsor is a mentor or guide who helps us grow and work through the 12 steps, keeping the focus on the sponsee.

The phone list is being passed around now. Feel free to add your name to the contact list at any time, and take anyone's name and contact info from the list at any time. Please indicate if you are interested in connecting in any of the above ways on the phone list.

If your group has newcomer liaisons/greeters

Please see .... (greeter/liaison name(s)) after the meeting to answer any questions you have about the ACA program, including working with another person to support your recovery. You may hear such people referred to as a sponsor, fellow traveler, co-sponsor, or recovery partner. This is a safe place to share our experiences and their effects on us today without judgment or criticism. We encourage members to share openly about their experiences. By regularly sharing in ACA meetings, we start to come out of denial and gain freedom from the effects of alcoholism and family dysfunction.

APPENDIX D—ONE MEMBER'S ACA SPONSORSHIP AGREEMENT

As fellow travelers, this sponsorship is based on reciprocity and honesty. I want to share my intentions and requests to support this being a safe sponsorship. I love having ACA in my life, and I'm excited to help others recover. It is said that "half measures availed us nothing." In ACA and other 12 step fellowships, we're afforded a "daily reprieve," which means we work our program daily. My support and guidance are conditional on your active participation in the ACA program.

I prefer to sponsor people who can attend at least one of my weekly in-person meetings and are able to meet me at my home until we finish the *Yellow Workbook*. If you relocate, we will need to discuss if and how we will continue our sponsorship relationship.

I will consistently fulfill these responsibilities as best I can:

- I will work the steps with you with gentleness, humor, love, and respect.

- I will share my experience, strength, and hope. Sometimes, I will offer suggestions, but it's your choice to take them on.

- I will keep our conversations confidential. I might speak with my sponsor or ACA counselor to get support to help me more effectively sponsor, but with no one else.

- I will be a fellow traveler primarily focused on recovery, both yours and mine, and consider friendship secondary to our healing. I prefer not to connect on social media until you've completed the 12 steps.

- I am available by phone to help you apply the program and be in The Solution.

- I will use my support network and take care of my needs; they are not your responsibility.

- I ask you to consistently fulfill these responsibilities as best you can:

- Attend ACA meetings consistently (at least once a week), read literature, attend to triggers, and contribute to the meeting through service. This involves helping as needed before, during, and after meetings and participating in business meetings. Meeting attendance and service are important parts of recovery that help us invest in our program and keep ACA alive.

- Meet with me regularly to work through the *Yellow Workbook* and apply reparenting. Schedule time with me when you've completed a step and are ready to discuss the related questions.

- Take full responsibility for your program (the *Big Red Book* p. 381).

- When you get stuck or notice parts of you avoiding ACA work or meetings, reach out. This happens! It is an opportunity to develop new, effective ways to live.

- If you want me to sponsor you after we conclude the *Yellow Workbook*, please stay in regular contact so I am familiar with your program, not just when you need support.

- Once you have completed step 12 with me, it's important to sponsor others. My sponsor always reminds me, "You've got to give it away to keep it." Sponsoring not only helps me stay committed to my recovery but also teaches me valuable lessons. It's incredibly rewarding to see someone work their program and make progress.

Sponsorship is a dynamic two-way street. We are both working the ACA program, but at different stages in our recovery. My role is to support you to apply the ACA program and be a guide for as long as it seems to be working. If any issues arise, I will bring them up, and I would appreciate it if you would do the same. At any point, we can pause and discuss the next steps to take.

Please note:

- This is an opportunity for us to each practice letting go of the traits, especially 1 (fear of people and authority figures), 2 (people-pleasing), 6 (overly-responsible), and 7 (guilt feelings standing up for our needs/self). Let's apply the program if our traits arise.

- Sponsees I've seen thrive in ACA have built an ACA support network with whom they are honest, real, and with whom they focus on being in The Solution.

- If you stop attending meetings, meeting with me for the steps, etc.,

I will ask you to get back on track. I sponsor people active in the program and who are all in. Other sponsors might ask less, but this is how I work.

- Sometimes, inner family members who aren't on board with doing ACA work show up, and we can experience avoidance or challenges to doing the work. Let me know if you notice this. I've not found it fruitful to proceed together until those parts are heard and supported by a professional.

- I keep Sundays free and don't answer calls. If it's urgent, please call and leave a message for a callback.

- From the *Big Red Book*: "A sponsor is not a parent, partner, guru, family member, authority figure, [therapist] or higher power to the person being sponsored." As adult children, some of us developed a habit of treating people as authority figures. If you find yourself seeking my approval or withholding information out of fear of being judged, please let me know. It can be a valuable opportunity for us to work through this together. You are the only authority for your program. I don't want to be seen as an authority figure; instead, I want to share my experience, strength, and hope (ESH) and help you discover your own inner authority.

Individuals recover at their own pace. These actions can help us apply the tools of recovery and reap the promises:

- Attend Meetings.
- Actively practice the 12 steps.
- Call program people to discuss recovery.
- Read ACA literature.
- Associate with recovering people.
- Define, set, and maintain boundaries.
- Build a personal support network.
- Actively make contact with the inner child.
- Service (in meetings, WSO, with sponsees, etc.)

Page 571 has more suggestions for ongoing recovery, including: stop acting out on food, sex, relationships, gambling, spending, or alcohol/drugs.

APPENDIX E—KEY RECOVERY GOALS AND MILESTONES

- Learn and grow in ability to have healthy relationships.
- Integrate, heal, or release survival traits.
- Reclaim our authentic selves.
- Feel a sense of wholeness, joy, and freedom.
- Transform our inner critical parent to an ally.
- Our inner child trusts us to handle life situations.
- Become comfortable with people, including authority figures.
- Develop a strong identity and generally approve of ourselves.
- Accept and use personal feedback to learn and grow.
- Become attracted by strengths and understand the weaknesses in our relationships with other people.
- Accept responsibility for our thoughts and actions.
- Feel comfortable standing up for ourselves when it is appropriate.
- Enjoy peace and serenity, trusting that a higher power is guiding our recovery.
- Love people who love and take care of themselves.
- Become free to feel and express our feelings even when they cause us pain.
- Develop a healthy sense of self-esteem.
- Initiate and complete ideas and projects.
- Consider alternative behaviors and possible consequences.
- Rely more and more on our higher power.
- Become active in service work.
- Become ready to help another in recovery work.
- Carry the message to another adult child.
- Learn to be gentle with ourselves and others.

- Keep the focus on "I," trying not to create unnecessary dramas or stories.
- Take care of ourselves and our inner children.
- Recognize when we are triggered, being self-compassionate and continuing to heal ourselves using our ACA recovery tools.
- Learn to say "No," and set boundaries.
- Trust ourselves and our decisions.
- Love ourselves unconditionally.

APPENDIX F—THE ACA PROMISES

1. We will discover our real identities by loving and accepting ourselves.
2. Our self-esteem will increase as we give ourselves approval on a daily basis.
3. Fear of authority figures and the need to people-please will leave us.
4. Our ability to share intimacy will grow inside us.
5. As we face our abandonment issues, we will be attracted by strengths and become more tolerant of weaknesses.
6. We will enjoy feeling stable, peaceful, and financially secure.
7. We will learn how to play and have fun in our lives.
8. We will choose to love people who can love and be responsible for themselves.
9. Healthy boundaries and limits will become easier for us to set.
10. Fears of failures and success will leave us, as we intuitively make healthier choices.
11. With help from our ACA support group, we will slowly release our dysfunctional behaviors.
12. Gradually, with our higher power's help, we learn to expect the best and get it.

APPENDIX G—THE ACA BILL OF RIGHTS

[Note: This document has completed fellowship review as of 2024 and is on the path to becoming ACA Conference Approved Literature.]

Many of us come into ACA not knowing that we could give ourselves permission to attend to our most basic needs. The journey of recovery in ACA can include learning to identify our needs, feelings, and rights, and to take responsibility for getting them met in a healthy fashion. At the same time, the rights we discover and determine for ourselves do not imply that others have the responsibility to fulfill those rights. With the help of these rights, we are able to develop healthier relationships, and with a power greater than ourselves of our own understanding, we can begin to live life as our True Selves.

1. I have the right to say no.
2. I have the right to say, "I don't know."
3. I have the right to be wrong.
4. I have the right to make mistakes and learn from them.
5. I have the right to detach from anyone in whose company I feel humiliated or manipulated.
6. I have the right to make my own choices and decisions in my life.
7. I have the right to grieve any actual or perceived loss.
8. I have the right to all of my feelings.
9. I have the right to feel angry, including towards someone I love.
10. I have the right to change my mind at any time.
11. I have the right to a spiritually, physically, and emotionally healthier existence, though it may differ entirely or in part from my parents' way of life.
12. I have the right to forgive myself and to choose how and when I forgive others.
13. I have the right to take healthy risks and to experiment with new possibilities.
14. I have the right to be honest in my relationships and to seek the same from others.

15. I have the right to ask for what I want.
16. I have the right to determine and honor my own priorities and goals and to allow others to do the same.
17. I have the right to dream and to have hope.
18. I have the right to be my True Self.
19. I have the right to know and nurture my inner child.
20. I have the right to laugh, to play, to have fun, and the freedom to celebrate this life—right here, right now.

APPENDIX H—HOW THE TRADITIONS GUIDE US IN WORKING WITH ANOTHER

ACA's Twelve Traditions provide guidance for ACA groups and our service structure. They are relevant to how we relate to each other on a one-to-one basis or in study groups. Here are the particular Traditions that relate to support relationships:

Tradition One

Our common welfare should come first; personal recovery depends on ACA unity.

This tradition reminds us that working with another person is based on the unity of our fellowship.

ACA unity is based on our similarities rather than our differences.

We are reminded to place the survival of our groups, whether meeting as two people or more than that, ahead of our selfish needs, or a fear-based urge to control others.

Problems can become opportunities to further our recovery, as we can learn to trust one another without being disagreeable.

We can have different viewpoints, but disagreements about what to do are measured by the principles of unity, and the most loving path to take.

We can speak up and express our views, all the while adding to ACA unity.

Tradition Two

For our group purpose, there is but one ultimate authority—a loving God as expressed in our group conscience. Our leaders are but trusted servants; they do not govern.

This Tradition reminds us that nobody in our support relationships can be an authority figure: Our higher power is the only authority as we work together.

While it is only natural that ACA's have a fear of authority figures or being authority figures, we remember that no one has authority over another in ACA recovery.

When we meet with a more experienced member, he or she leads by example but learns from the newer person as well.

When we give and receive support in groups, we can hold group conscience discussions to provide a spiritual method by which a higher power is expressed in our decisions.

Tradition Nine

ACA, as such, ought never be organized, but we may create service boards or committees directly responsible to those they serve.

This tradition reminds us that our "support relationship" is different from our dysfunctional childhood relationships.

Tradition Twelve

Anonymity is the spiritual foundation of all our Traditions, ever reminding us to place principles before personalities.

This Tradition reminds us to maintain anonymity in our support relationships, whether supporting or being supported.

When we maintain each other's confidentiality, we give each other the opportunity to break the "don't talk" rule within the relationship. We do not talk about each other's stories or share outside the relationship, even with good intentions.

With the promise of anonymity, we can feel comfortable telling our story.

By placing principles before personalities, we are guided by what ACA is teaching us as we resolve differences if they arise, and this keeps us all safe.

The guidance about confidentiality does not apply to protecting an abuser: We retain the right to speak out if the relationship has become unsafe in any way.

APPENDIX I—ACA SUGGESTED COMMITMENT TO SERVICE

I perform service so that my program will be available for myself, and through those efforts, others may benefit. I will perform service and practice my recovery by:

1. Affirming that the true power of our program rests in the membership of the meetings and is expressed through our higher power and through group conscience.

2. Confirming that our process is one of inclusion and not exclusion; showing special sensitivity to the viewpoint of the minority in the process of formulating the group conscience so that any decision is reflective of the spirit of the group and not merely the vote of the majority.

3. Placing principles before personalities.

4. Keeping myself fit for service by working my recovery as a member of the program.

5. Striving to facilitate the sharing of experience, strength, and hope at all levels: meetings, Intergroups, Regional committees, service boards, and World Services.

6. Accepting the different forms and levels of service and allowing those around me to each function according to their own abilities.

7. Remaining willing to forgive myself and others for not performing perfectly.

8. Being willing to surrender the position in which I serve in the interest of unity and to provide the opportunity for others to serve; to avoid problems of money, property, and prestige; and to avoid losing my own recovery through service to act out my old behavior, especially in taking care of others, controlling, rescuing, being a victim, etc.

9. Remembering I am a trusted servant; I do not govern.

APPENDIX J—SAFETY TENT CARD

Preventing Unsafe Behavior in ACA. ACA has one primary purpose: to carry the message to adult children who still suffer. When unsafe behavior occurs in and around meetings, we are distracted from this purpose.

Any person seeking healing from childhood trauma is welcome at this group. If any person endangers another individual or disrupts the group's efforts to carry the ACA message, the group will take action appropriate to the situation. Anonymity is an important principle of 12 step recovery; however, anonymity in meetings does not shield anyone from accountability when unsafe or illegal behavior occurs. To protect the common welfare of this group and our fellowship, unsafe or illegal behavior will not be tolerated.

Addressing such behavior can include asking someone to leave the meeting, calling a group conscience to discuss the situation, and contacting the proper authorities should the situation require it.

Your personal recovery is too important to remain in a meeting that does not work for you. Check out other meetings to find one that does work for you.

For more information about preventing unsafe behavior in ACA, please see the booklet entitled, "Why We Need to Talk About Predatory Behavior," available for free download at http://adultchildren.org/wp-content/uploads/2019/02/Predatory_Behavior_ComLine_Final.pdf

APPENDIX K—INTRODUCTION TO ACA WORKGROUPS

[Note: This is taken from *A New Hope.*]

In ACA, we embrace various approaches to doing deeper recovery work with others in the program. Whether our focus is the 12 steps, reparenting work in the *Loving Parent Guidebook*, or exploring and healing our adaptive childhood traits in the *Laundry Lists Workbook*, ACA recognizes that different approaches work well for different people at different times. Historically, in most 12 step programs, people do concentrated recovery work one-to-one (traditionally using a sponsor/sponsee model). In ACA, adult children have explored alternative approaches to doing intensive recovery work, including being part of small, private workgroups, both in person and online.

Doing one-to-one work can be challenging for some adult children. Growing up in our dysfunctional home environments, we learned not to talk or feel… and we learned not to *trust*. In the absence of trust, many adult children developed a fear of authority in childhood (*Traits 1 & 3*), a desire to seek approval from those in authority (*Trait 2*), or reflexive reactions to fight against authority (*Other Traits*). Some of us tried to protect ourselves by using the power of authority and control against others (*Other Traits*). Therefore, some adult children can struggle with asking for, receiving, and offering support through one-to-one recovery relationships. ACA workgroups can sometimes help mitigate these dynamics.

However, workgroups can present challenges, too. Laundry lists traits behaviors can still arise, and members can trigger one another. While recovery requires us to stretch to try new things and work with discomfort, we need a basic sense of safety to recover. We might realize that a particular group isn't a match or that group work isn't a good fit for us at the time. It's OK to leave groups that don't work for us and find ones that do. Finding a workgroup that fits is a process and can take time.

The workgroup model can be a particularly powerful healing format for adult children. Our original wounding occurred within a dysfunctional family, so it makes sense that we might find profound healing in a small workgroup with members of our ACA family. Communal attunement and consistent connection from a group of trusted others can be transformative in our recovery process. ACA workgroups can provide what the *Big Red Book* calls "indirect sponsorship," and gradually, we might come to trust and rely on the group conscience for support and guidance. In time, members of our workgroup can form the foundation for our recovery support network... each a vital source of individual experience, strength, and hope.

CREATING / JOINING ACA WORKGROUPS

Duration

The ACA workgroup model usually involves working through an entire workbook as a group (*Twelve Steps, Loving Parent Guidebook, Laundry Lists Workbook*, etc.). This format allows each participant to address all written text, questions, and exercises contained within. Completing a workbook can take anywhere from several months to over a year, depending on the pace. Most groups meet weekly for between one and two hours. Discussing time commitments up-front can help clarify individual needs and intentions as the workgroup is forming. These issues may need to be re-addressed as the group progresses and finds its own pace.

Group Size

Workgroup sizes usually range from between four and twelve members. Participants determine together what size group will work best. Newly forming workgroups sometimes stay open for the first few weeks, allowing new members to join. At some mutually agreed-upon point, the workgroup "closes" to new members. It is not uncommon for some participants to discontinue attending the group for various reasons, decreasing the workgroup size over time.

Location

The group must identify a safe and consistent place to meet each week. Usually, in-person workgroups meet in the home of one of the participants. Alternative locations might include non-profit centers with private meeting spaces, such as hospitals, places of worship, or 12 step clubhouses. Online workgroups will need to identify a platform (such as Zoom, Facebook, Teams, Hangouts, Skype, etc.) and who will have access to and be responsible for starting and hosting meetings. It's important to develop contingencies if the person hosting the meeting (either in person or online) can't make it or doesn't show.

Format

The process of going through any of the ACA workbooks will involve *reading, writing, sharing, and witnessing*. Groups may choose to **read** through the large text sections in the workbook together, taking turns and pausing for discussion. Or workgroups may agree to read sections ahead of time on their own and come prepared to discuss. **Writing** can involve answering questions or doing other types of written exercises. It is suggested that participants do the written sections ahead of time on their own. However, most workgroups don't *require* anyone to do this type of "homework." Most groups read sequentially through all questions together, allowing each participant to **share** their responses or pass. Finally, **witnessing** is one of the most important parts of the ACA workgroup healing process. Participants quietly and attentively listen as each member courageously breaks the old rules of family dysfunction: d*on't talk, don't trust, don't feel.*

Safety Guidelines

New workgroups are encouraged to create safety agreements. Some groups write out guidelines; others do not. Topics may include time/duration commitments to the group, attendance & missing meetings, phone/electronics use, alcohol/drug/food use, crosstalk & fixing, sharing time limits, confidentiality, etc. Safety guidelines can be revisited and adjusted if group member needs change.

Experience & Expertise

Having one or more people in a workgroup with previous ACA workgroup experience can be beneficial. However, including a "veteran" participant isn't always possible, nor is having a more experienced member required (nor sometimes even desired). Anyone in ACA can start a workgroup. There are no workgroup "experts" or "authorities" in ACA.

Questions, Conflict & Authority

ACA workgroups can help ease authority-related laundry lists traits effects for some people. Still, authority issues in group work, just like in one-to-one work, can and do surface. Some adult children seek to make others an authority who will "give them all the answers." Others reflexively react with hostility if they feel someone is telling them what to do. Some adult children protect themselves by trying to assert control in authoritative ways. When questions and conflicts arise, participants are encouraged to address them together openly, honestly, and directly. Resolving conflict in the spirit of the workgroup's safety guidelines, adhering to ACA Traditions, and with as much gentleness, patience, love, and respect as possible can be healing and empowering. To support group safety, participants are encouraged to ask ACA fellow travelers outside the workgroup for their experience, strength, and hope *in ways that do not breach the workgroup's confidentiality*. Addressing disagreement and conflict can be challenging for adult children. Yet, it can also be an opportunity to deepen one's growth and recovery process.

For 12 Step Work – Other Laundry List Use

The other laundry list traits were more formally developed after the *Twelve Steps Yellow Workbook* was created. Some workgroups choose to include this information in their 12 Step work. If a group wishes, the other laundry list traits can be referenced whenever the standard laundry list traits are presented throughout the *ACA Twelve Step Yellow Workbook*.

For 12 Step Work – Tony A's 12 Steps Use

Tony A's version of the 12 steps is not in the *Yellow Workbook* due to copyright issues. Still, some workgroups choose to include this information in their 12 Step work. A group can decide to introduce and reference Tony A's version of the 12 steps when the standard ACA 12 steps are referenced in the *ACA Twelve Step Yellow Workbook*.

Additional Workgroup Resources for the *Loving Parent Guidebook*

Available at https://adultchildren.org/literature/loving-parent-guidebook/

ACA WORKGROUP
SAMPLE SAFETY GUIDELINES

The following are some **sample** safety suggestions. Each workgroup determines for itself what guidelines to put in place to support safety. Guidelines can be revisited and modified over time.

- Please arrive on time to be considerate of other group members. Members agree to notify at least one other participant ahead of time if they will not be attending a workgroup meeting. Regular attendance is recommended.*

- Please do not attend workgroup meetings if under the influence of illicit substances or alcohol.

- Please silence (preferably turn off) and put away electronic devices upon arrival to reduce possibilities for distraction and interruption.

- Please be mindful of equitable sharing times, allowing all participants equal opportunities to share. A three-minute-per-share limit (with some exceptions now and then) is recommended.**

- Please respect participants' freedom to pass and share at the level that feels comfortable to them.

- Please do not interrupt other members when they are sharing.

- Please use the words "I, me, and my" to share from your personal experience.

- Please do not "cross-talk," which for this group means not referring to, commenting directly on, or judging/criticizing anyone else's sharing. We simply listen and do not offer advice. Attentively listening to others as they face their pain can often be the greatest support of all.

- Please respect the privacy of those who share. What is communicated at our workgroup meeting stays at this meeting.

* Long absences may threaten workgroup safety. Therefore, some groups choose to set specific boundaries around attendance, such as limits on consecutive absences or the total number of workgroup meetings missed.

** Some groups time participant shares for various lengths of time. Others do not.